DEMYSTIFYING TAX FOR THE COMMON MAN

CA VIREN RAJANI

Notion Press

No.8, 3rd Cross Street,
CIT Colony, Mylapore,
Chennai, Tamil Nadu – 600004

First Published by Notion Press 2020
Copyright © CA Viren Rajani 2020
All Rights Reserved.

ISBN 978-1-63669-506-8

This book has been published with all efforts taken to make the material error-free after the consent of the author. However, the author and the publisher do not assume and hereby disclaim any liability to any party for any loss, damage, or disruption caused by errors or omissions, whether such errors or omissions result from negligence, accident, or any other cause.

While every effort has been made to avoid any mistake or omission, this publication is being sold on the condition and understanding that neither the author nor the publishers or printers would be liable in any manner to any person by reason of any mistake or omission in this publication or for any action taken or omitted to be taken or advice rendered or accepted on the basis of this work. For any defect in printing or binding the publishers will be liable only to replace the defective copy by another copy of this work then available.

This book has been updated for latest amendments.

PRAISE FOR THE BOOK

"Viren's 'Demystifying Tax' is simple and pragmatic - words not usually associated with the world of taxation. A practical understanding of tax is critical for each of us. And I would recommend this as a must read for any taxpayer."

– Nimisha Jain,
Managing Director & Partner, Boston Consulting Group

"The book succinctly summarises the basics of taxation in a simple yet lucid style. It's a must read for anyone keen to understand the what's and why's of the subject. I wish you all the best for a successful publication and hope this is the first of many more to come from your table."

– CA Divakar Vijayasarathy,
Managing Partner, DVS Advisors

"This book effortlessly highlights the basics of tax such that it is easy for any beginner to consume and interesting for any experienced individual to be hooked on to, two elements I try to incorporate in every class I teach."

– Mr. Seshadrinath,
HOD, B. Com Honours, DG Vaishnav College, Chennai

"If you find yourself googling complex Indian tax laws for a query or are simply looking for a better understanding of the tax system – go for this simple read! It is especially a must have for early professionals / businesspersons to be aware of tax basics at different stages of their career."

– Pulkit Jain,
Director – Strategy, Glance

"The book has been penned vehemently, also keeping in mind the intricacies and complexities involved in the subject. The cogent approach has made it an intriguing piece to read, touching the basics beautifully. A "go-to" guide for the ones who want to appreciate the fundamentals of tax"

– CA Jugal Gala,
Associate Principal – Research, DVS Advisors

"This book stands true to its name – if you're someone who finds tax books complicated or cumbersome to read through, be sure to give this a shot regardless of your background."

– CA Divyansh Jain (AIR 10, Nov 2018)

"Simple and easy-to-comprehend, this book comes as a solution point for beginners looking to take a peek into the taxation world."

– CA Salonee Kabra (AIR 24, May 2019)

"Demystifying Tax has got the right balance of details and overall implications for anybody seeking to understand the basics of tax well."

– CA Simran Shah (AIR 23, May 2019)

With the deepest gratitude to

Mom and Dad

It's impossible to thank you adequately for everything you've done, from loving me unconditionally to raising me in a stable household, where you instilled the best values and taught me to celebrate and embrace life.

All my mentors

For showing me the right path, encouraging me to push the envelope and supporting me throughout this journey. I consider it my extreme good fortune to have you in my life.

The Almighty

For teaching me to hope, giving me the strength to never give up and answering my prayers.

CONTENTS

Foreword 11

Preface 13

Why This Book? 15

1. **FUNDAMENTALS OF TAXATION** 17
    - 1.1 What is 'tax'? 17
    - 1.2 Why does the government need to levy tax? 18
    - 1.3 How does the government collect tax? 20
    - 1.4 Who does the tax burden fall on? 26
    - 1.5 Recent taxation trends in India 28
    - 1.6 Key takeaways 34

2. **ORGANIZATION OF THE TAX SYSTEM IN INDIA** ... 35
    - 2.1 Introduction 35
    - 2.2 Know your tax authorities 35
    - 2.3 Your tax authorities have a hierarchy too 36
    - 2.4 Ensuring your honesty – information sources used by the IT department 38
    - 2.5 Consultants to the government – TPRU and TPC ... 42
    - 2.6 Key takeaways 44

3. ELEMENTAL TAX KNOWLEDGE FOR A SALARIED PERSON 45

   3.1 Introduction 45

   3.2 What does my 'salary' include? 45

   3.3 How is my salary taxed? 48

   3.4 What is the rate at which my salary is taxed? 49

   3.5 How can I reduce the tax incidence on my salary income? 50

   3.6 The choice between different tax regimes 60

   3.7 Key takeaways 62

4. ELEMENTAL TAX KNOWLEDGE FOR AN ENTREPRENEUR 63

   4.1 Introduction 63

   4.2 Why is business income taxed? 64

   4.3 What does 'business income' include? 66

   4.4 How is business income taxed? 68

   4.5 Treading with caution 84

   4.6 Key takeaways 86

5. OTHER INCOMES THAT DEMAND ATTENTION 87

   5.1 Introduction 87

   5.2 Other incomes that demand attention – an overview 87

   5.3 Direct taxes related to your house 89

   5.4 Direct taxes related to your investments 92

	5.5	Incomes you need not pay tax on	97
	5.6	Are your gifts also taxed?	98
	5.7	Gaining from your losses	99
	5.8	Be careful of other taxes too	100
	5.9	Key takeaways	104
6.	**TAX COMPLIANCES**	**105**
	6.1	Introduction	105
	6.2	Direct tax compliances	105
	6.3	Indirect tax compliances	129
	6.4	Key takeaways	134

About the Author *135*

FOREWORD

In the course of more than 26 years that I have been with the Income Tax department, I have come across hundreds of queries on tax-related matters. As you would imagine, they form a wide spectrum, from a disputed gift to a corporate merger. But at the end of the day, there is always a simple, elegant answer for any situation. I have met select experts who have the ability to look beyond the obvious and generate insights to solve any problem - Viren is one such person.

I have known him for more than 5 years and have witnessed first-hand his ability to break down problems into clear concepts to see the big picture. This book is his attempt to replicate his biggest strength: simplify the behemoth that is our tax system into an easy-to-digest format.

'Demystifying Tax for The Common Man' is one of the few books to lay out basic tax concepts that one should be abreast with, which may seem complicated, in a way that's easy to read and understand. To all readers who have ever faced a tax-related query and found themselves reaching out for the guidance of a tax expert or simply searching for a cure online - update yourself with the trove of information here! If you're just looking out for what taxation in our country is like, this is a good place to start as well. With this book as your guide, you are one step away from being demystified about taxation in India.

– Aruna Anandraj
Assistant Commissioner of Income Tax (ACIT)
Income Tax Department, Government of India

PREFACE

Like every other CA aspirant, I spent majority of my student life working as an Articled Assistant as part of a three-year long internship. During my articleship, I came across many entrepreneurs who arrived at my firm with a tax notice in their hand (or email, depending on the client), in fear at the thought of paying more tax. And so, a considerable amount of time was spent in breaking down and simplifying the problem for them. Then again, it was fair, right? They weren't expected to understand tax in-depth, that's where we CAs are supposed to help them. I wished I could help more such people, but my efforts were limited to those who arrived at our doorstep.

Later, as I became a senior, many students, both CA aspirants and others, would also come to me for advice on pursuing this course, or simply wanting to learn more about major subjects like tax. Textbooks could only tell them so much about theory, they remained unaware about practicalities of this course. Their curiosity about taxation was heartening, and as I put their basics in place, their problem-solving abilities improved manifold. I wanted to help many others like them in demystifying taxation.

Taxation is a topic that is at the epicenter of public life in India. Yet, there are complaints about taxes being complicated, difficult to understand and an object of fear. Addressing these complaints was the primary impetus behind this book. It is in the spirit of learning about tax, breaking down complex problems in an easy-to-digest form and dispelling the fear surrounding taxation that I bring forth this book. It is not intended to be a plain language translation of our tax system. Rather, I have written it with a hope that those students, entrepreneurs and many more people find value in these pages and are able to apply the same to their own lives.

WHY THIS BOOK?

Before going ahead with writing this book, we thought to validate our initial theory on whether there is an actual need for the book. And so, we surveyed 1,767 people across Mumbai, Delhi, Chennai, Kolkata, Bangalore and Ahmedabad from different fields - students, chartered accountants, lawyers, entrepreneurs, etc. to get the public opinion.

I'd like to share the results and key insights from our survey below:

Of the people surveyed,

1. ~**40%** did not have a basic idea about tax
2. ~**41%** expressed curiosity to learn more about tax
3. ~**25%** expressed a need for simple and structured content on tax

This research gave our belief a scientific backing. We decided to go ahead and write something that could be of use to professionals/ entrepreneurs who fear the unknown, curious readers who crave basics and those who need simple and structured content to learn more about tax.

• CHAPTER 1 •

FUNDAMENTALS OF TAXATION

1.1 What is 'tax'?

We all know what tax means, right? It goes by many names – tariff, levy, duty, toll, cess, etc., all meaning the same thing. It is money we pay to the government once we start earning it. In effect, it is the cost of living in a society, imposed by both, Central and State governments in different forms.

But do we really know how taxation works? As soon as I became a Chartered Accountant, I had innumerable people come up to me and tell me *"Now that you are a CA, I can ask you all my tax doubts (and you can file my returns)"*. I realized that most people are unaware about even basic tax-related things one ought to know. And whenever you don't know something, you end up fearing that very thing. That is what tax in India has become, since a vast majority of people are not aware about, and thus fear, complex tax laws of the country.

It's not just about income tax, although that one affects us the most. We hear about a plethora of taxes – income tax, wealth tax, tax on imports, and a fairly recent tax – goods and services tax (or 'GST'), among many others. These taxes have become a regular aspect of our lives – every time we buy food from the supermarket, pay rent to the landlord, or get a salary credit lower than what we expected. Thus, it is necessary to understand the 'What, Why and How?' of taxation in India and remove the fear around it.

This book is intended to help with these basics, but to learn and master tax, a bigger perspective is needed. A perspective that will come not just from the sections of Income Tax Act and its rules, but a comprehensive understanding of Acts, Rules, guidance notes, circulars, notifications and case laws of both direct and indirect taxes.

1.2 Why does the government need to levy tax?

But why does the government need my money?

A government's role is to ensure the welfare of a nation, i.e. look after its citizens' various interests, such as construction of roads and bridges, health facilities, schools and provision of social services like national security, provision of salaries for civil servants including the police, army, judges, doctors, nurses, teachers and many more. It is interesting to note how the central government spends the money at their disposal (Exhibits 1A and 1B). Interest payments account for little less than one-fourth of the total expenditure budget. Balance includes spend on defense, food subsidies, agricultural welfare, education (human resource development) and road transport among others.

In order to fund these expenses, the government needs to source money from various tools in its arsenal – taxes from the community, dividends and profits from its investments, rendering services, etc. In the event these are not enough to cover its expenditures, the government must borrow money or sell its share of investments. In FY 2020-21, >50% expenditures are estimated to be funded by tax revenues (Exhibit 2).

As such, the purpose of taxation is to increase a country's productivity since capital is allocated by the government into projects that will boost socio-economic development. Taxes can also be used to prevent intake of certain socially undesirable items, such as tobacco, alcohol, etc. By levying taxes, consumers can be discouraged from buying these products due to higher prices. Governments also use taxes to protect their local industry from external competition by imposing taxes on imported goods and making them more expensive.

EXHIBIT 1A | GOVERNMENT SPENDS ITS REVENUES ON DEBT-SERVICE COSTS (INTEREST PAYMENTS), COMMUNITY, SOCIAL & ECONOMIC DEVELOPMENT, GENERAL PUBLIC SERVICES, PEACE & SECURITY, HEALTH, LEARNING & CULTURE

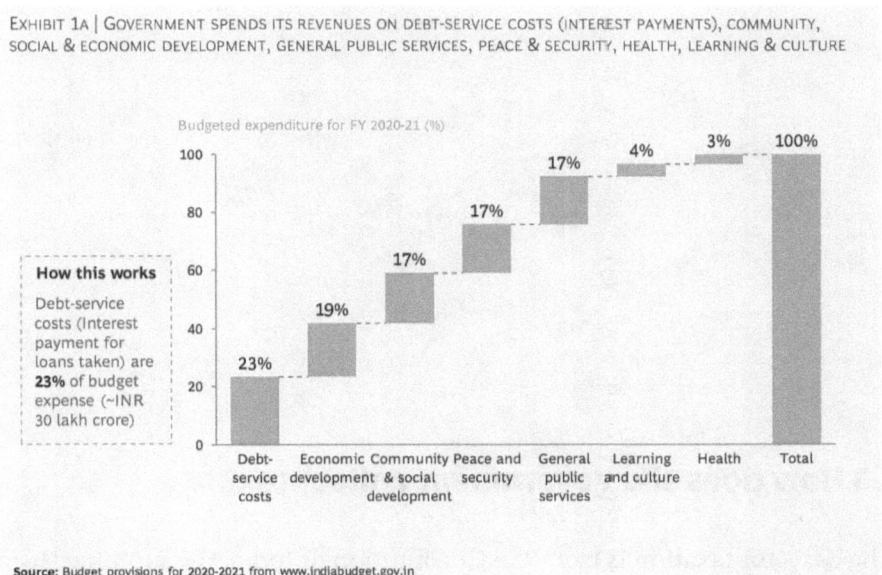

Source: Budget provisions for 2020-2021 from www.indiabudget.gov.in

EXHIBIT 1B | GOVERNMENT SPENDS ITS REVENUES ON DEBT-SERVICE COSTS (INTEREST PAYMENTS), COMMUNITY, SOCIAL & ECONOMIC DEVELOPMENT, GENERAL PUBLIC SERVICES, PEACE & SECURITY, HEALTH, LEARNING & CULTURE

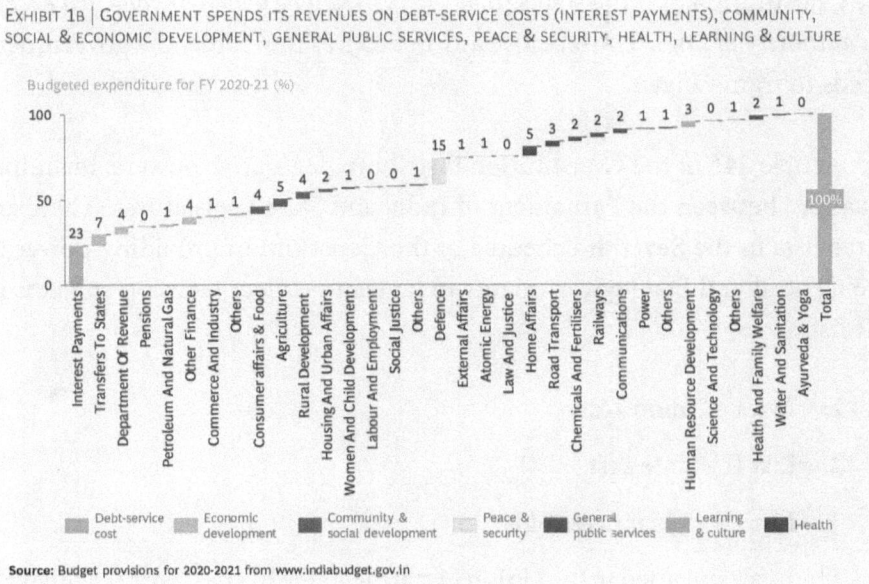

Source: Budget provisions for 2020-2021 from www.indiabudget.gov.in

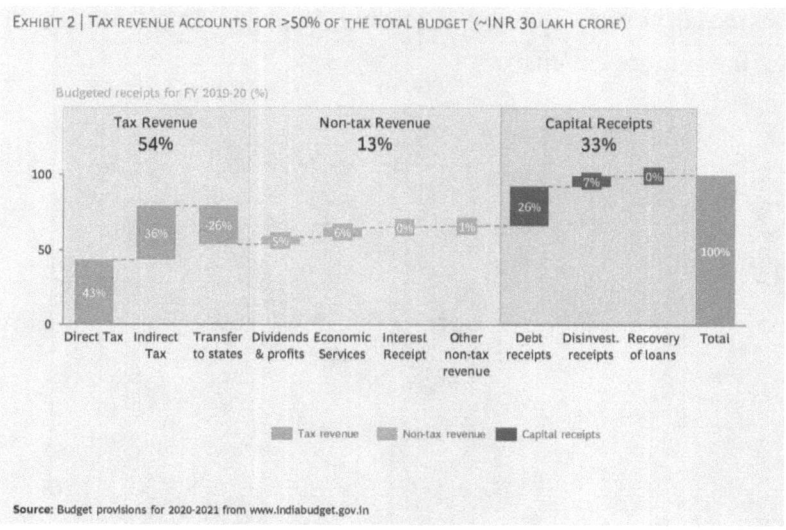

1.3 How does the government collect tax?

The basis for taxation is from the Constitution of India, the supreme law of land. All other laws are secondary to the Constitution of India. Article 265 of the Constitution of India states that *"No tax shall be levied or collected except by authority of law"*. Thus, before any tax comes into force, the government needs to frame a law.

Article 246 of the Constitution distributes legislative powers, including taxation, between the Parliament of India and State Legislatures. There are three lists in the Seventh Schedule of the Constitution providing power to the Central and State governments to levy and collect taxes on subjects in the lists:

1. List I - Union List
2. List II - State List
3. List III - Concurrent List

The taxes specified in the Union List are leviable by the Centre exclusively while those listed in the States List are leviable by the state exclusively. The

Concurrent List includes subjects on which both, the Parliament & State Legislatures, have the power to make laws. They exercise their power by levying two types of taxes – direct tax and indirect tax.

On one hand, direct taxes are those which are paid directly to the government by those on whom they are imposed. Income tax, for instance, is the most popular direct tax. The person paying direct taxes cannot recover them from somebody else.

On the other hand, when the person on whom tax is levied passes the burden on to someone else, that tax is called an indirect tax. For example, GST paid by a restaurant to the government is ultimately passed on to the customer enjoying the food as a charge on their total bill. It is collected by an intermediary (the restaurant) and passed on to the government.

Direct Taxes

Key direct taxes in India include the following:

1. **Income Tax:** As the name suggests, income tax is a charge on various types of income. The law governing the same in India is the Income Tax Act, 1961, along with the Rules set by this act.

    The definition of income, however, includes not just 'salary'. It also covers any income from rent of house property, profits or gains from any business or profession, gain on sale of capital assets, such as land, house, shares, etc. and any other sources of income. The latter is a residual category that covers multiple incomes like lottery winnings, interest income on any loans extended, gains due to speculation, etc.

2. **Wealth Tax:** This was imposed up until 1 April 2016, wherein every individual, company or Hindu Undivided Family (we will come to this in a short while) which had net wealth exceeding INR 30 lakhs had to pay tax on the excess to the extent of 1%. Since then, this has been substituted by a surcharge (another tax) on the taxes paid by high-income generators.

3. **Securities Transaction Tax:** Also called STT, this is a tax levied every time you purchase or sell a share. All securities traded on Indian stock exchanges have this tax affixed with them at the time of each trading transaction.

4. **Corporate Taxes:** In addition to income tax, a company also pays Minimum Alternate Tax (MAT) and Dividend Distribution Tax (DDT).

    a. **MAT:** Essentially, MAT is levied for companies to pay a minimum tax (currently at 15%) and limit the exemptions availed by companies. Hence, most companies must calculate two kinds of taxes on their income – normal tax liability and MAT liability. Once MAT is paid, the company can take the credit of excess MAT paid forward and claim it in any year the company's normal tax liability is higher than its MAT liability.

    b. **DDT:** Dividends are payments made by a company to its shareholders, as distribution of its profits. On such a distribution, companies would earlier pay DDT at 15% on the gross dividend amount. This dividend income would be tax-free in the hands of investors (up to INR 10 lakhs, post which the excess would be taxed at 10%). However, the recent Budget 2020 has abolished DDT. This means that distributing companies are no longer required to deduct DDT and shareholders must pay tax on dividends as per their own slab rates.

Indirect Taxes

Taxes levied on goods and services are indirect taxes. Since they are imposed on a product and not the income of a person, an intermediary, i.e. the individual selling the product or providing service collects them. Unlike direct taxes, these are regressive in nature because they are not based on the principle of 'ability to pay'. All consumers, even the economically challenged, bear the burden of indirect taxes equally.

Earlier, several indirect taxes were levied in India – excise duty, customs duty, service tax, central sales tax, value added tax (VAT), entry tax, purchase tax, entertainment tax, tax on lottery, betting and gambling, luxury tax, tax on advertisements, etc.

However, the indirect tax regime in India witnessed a shift on 1 July 2017, when many Central and State taxes were merged into a single tax, i.e. Goods and Services Tax (GST). Of the above, customs duty continues in the post-GST era, while these taxes have been subsumed in GST (Exhibit 3).

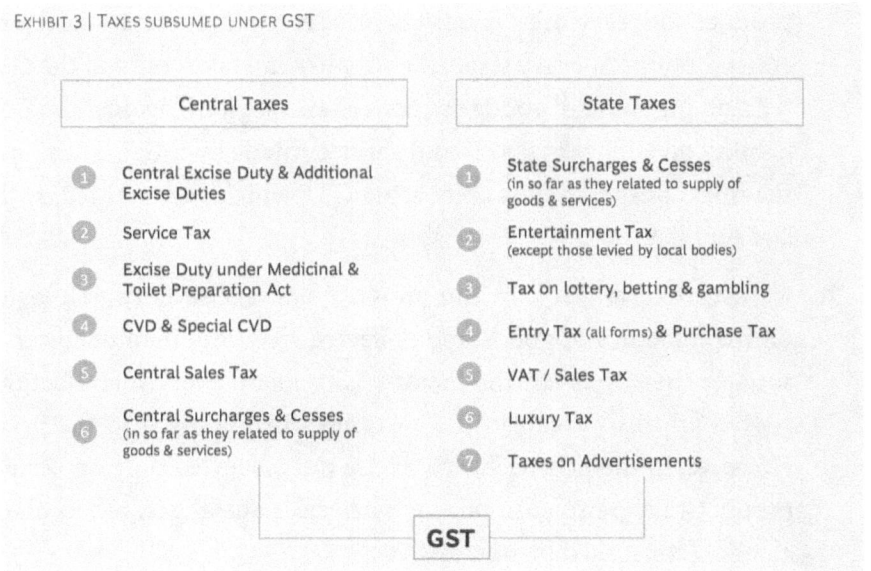

EXHIBIT 3 | TAXES SUBSUMED UNDER GST

It has been a long road to getting GST where it is, one which took 17 years to fruition (Exhibit 4).

Exhibit 4

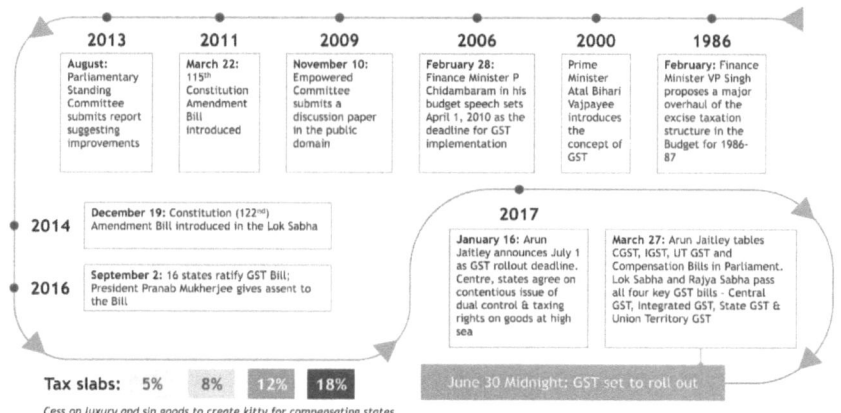

GST's 17-year roller coaster ride to final rollout

Source: Moneycontrol (PTI Graphics)

1. **GST:** It is a 'value added tax', which is levied on each stage of a product or service's value chain, i.e. manufacture, sale and consumption. At every stage, the supplier can take credit of the GST paid on purchase of goods or services and set it off against the GST liability on supply of goods and services made by them. Thus, only the final consumer ends up bearing GST which was charged by the last supplier.

2. **Central Excise duty:** In the pre-GST era, excise duty was levied on manufacture of goods and collected from the manufacturer as soon as the goods left the factory. Ultimately, every manufacturer passed on this burden to the customers by adding it to the price. However, in the post-GST era, excise duty is levied only on certain products, i.e. petroleum products, diesel, natural gas, tobacco and alcohol (consumed by humans).

3. **Customs duty:** Every time you purchase something from outside India, you are charged an additional customs duty on the same. The intention is to ensure that the goods being brought into India are taxed the same way as goods manufactured in India, and domestic goods are not at a disadvantage. In certain cases, customs duty is also levied on export of goods from India.

   Earlier, an additional charge known as 'Countervailing duty (CVD)' was levied on imports to compensate for the excise duty charged on locally manufactured goods, and 'Special CVD' was levied on imports in lieu of the erstwhile local sales tax. However, after the introduction of GST, CVD and Special CVD have been replaced by a GST component.

4. **Value Added Tax (VAT):** As the name suggests, VAT was a tax levied on the value added at each stage of manufacture or distribution of products, finally shifting the tax burden to the end-customer. However, after GST's introduction, there are very few goods left under the purview of VAT, such as petroleum products, diesel, alcohol (consumed by humans) and natural gas.

5. **Service tax:** Just like there was VAT for goods, there was Service tax for services. Every time one person rendered a service to another person, e.g. using Vodafone's mobile network, the service provider would charge a service tax to the recipient and be liable to remit the same to the government. However, GST brought together goods and services to make 'one tax for one nation'.

You might wonder – the definition of VAT is like that of GST. Then why go through the hassle and bring in a whole new tax? Despite the principle of value-added taxation existing in India, this was separate at the Central and State level, i.e. excise duty at a central level and VAT at the state level. Credit of excise duty paid (CENVAT) could not be set off against liability of VAT levied at the State level. This led to double taxation since when goods were manufactured and sold, VAT would be charged even on the excise duty component. Moreover, the difference between a 'good' and a 'service' was often blurred. E.g. software was liable to both VAT and service tax. Further, several local level taxes, such as luxury tax, entertainment tax, etc., were not included in VAT.

GST addressed the above-mentioned problems and more. Indirect taxes are integrated at the Central and State level, and major indirect taxes have been subsumed into GST.

1.4 Who does the tax burden fall on?

If we look at income tax, Section 4 of the Income Tax Act lays down the basic 'charge' of Income tax, i.e. income tax for any year is to be charged as per provisions of the Income Tax Act. This charge of taxes is on 'persons'. This is not to be confused to mean an individual. Every person listed below is treated as a separate tax entity under the Income Tax Act (Exhibit 5A).

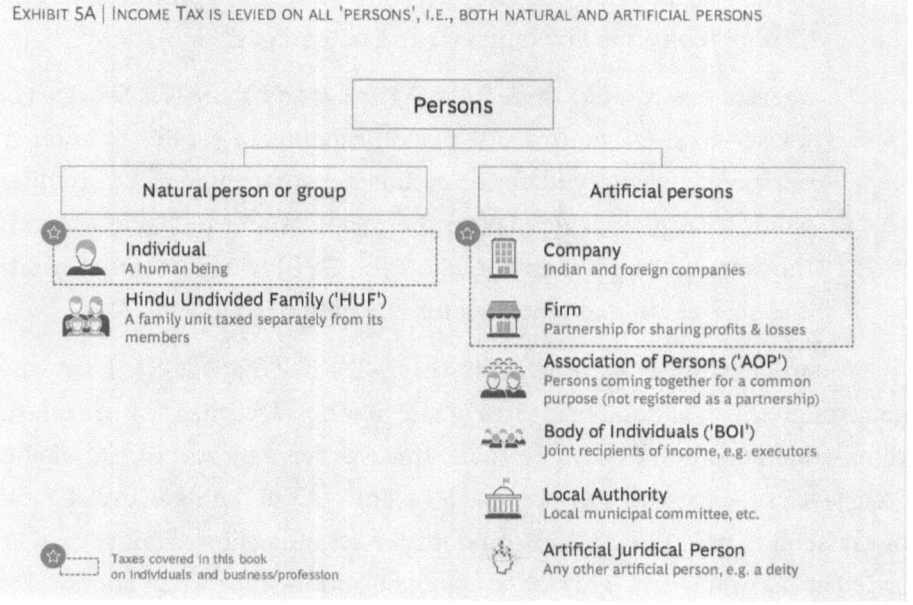

EXHIBIT 5A | INCOME TAX IS LEVIED ON ALL 'PERSONS', I.E., BOTH NATURAL AND ARTIFICIAL PERSONS

However, even within persons, there is a difference between persons who are 'residents' and 'citizens' and tax systems around the world vary on this aspect. Most countries, such as India, tax income on a residency basis – which means residents are taxed on their worldwide income, while some countries like Singapore follow 'territorial' system of taxation where income derived by Residents from outside Singapore is not taxed. On the other hand, there are exceptions like the United States which taxes its 'citizens' as residents.

Let's understand India's take on this a little better – are all individual residents and their income taxed the same way? How do you even know if you are a resident or not? These answers are in Exhibit 5B.

Exhibit 5B | Determining the residential status of an individual and scope of taxing their income

Status	Definition	Income taxed
① Resident	Stays in India for • **182 days** or more in that year; or • **365 days** or more in last **4 years** and **60 days**[1] or more in that year **Deemed resident:** Indian citizen with total income (Indian sourced) >Rs. 15 lakhs and not liable to tax in any other country	Global income: • Income **earned in India**; and • Income **earned outside India**
② Resident – Not Ordinarily Resident (RNOR)	A Resident (fulfilling the above) who: • has been a NR in **9 out of 10** previous years; or • has been in India for **729 days** or less in last **7 years** **By Finance Act 2020:** • Indian citizen / PIO with total income >Rs.15 lakhs (Indian sourced) with ≥120 days, <182 days • Deemed resident mentioned above	Income **earned in India**. Tax need not be paid in India on their foreign income[2]
③ Non-Resident (NR)	Person who is **not a resident** in India i.e. doesn't fulfill conditions under (1)	Income **earned in India** (not foreign income)

1. Exception: When an Indian citizen leaves India for employment in a year, or POI being outside comes for a visit, they will be a Resident if they stay in India for 182 days or more. But if their total income (Indian sourced) > Rs 15 lakh, this period is reduced to 120 days or more
2. Unless it is derived from a business controlled in or a profession set up in India

In this book, we will address the tax implications of major taxes on individuals and businesses:

Taxes on an individual

As an individual working a job, the primary source of income is your **'salary'**. Individuals pay income tax on salary to the government regularly. It is important to understand how salary is taxed in India, who is asked to contribute what portion of their income and what are the ways in which you can save on this tax.

Taxes on a business or profession

Primary taxes paid by a business or professional include **income tax and indirect taxes,** i.e. Income tax, GST, etc. among others.

1.5 Recent taxation trends in India

India's tax-to-GDP ratio is on the lower side when compared to major economies (Exhibit 6).

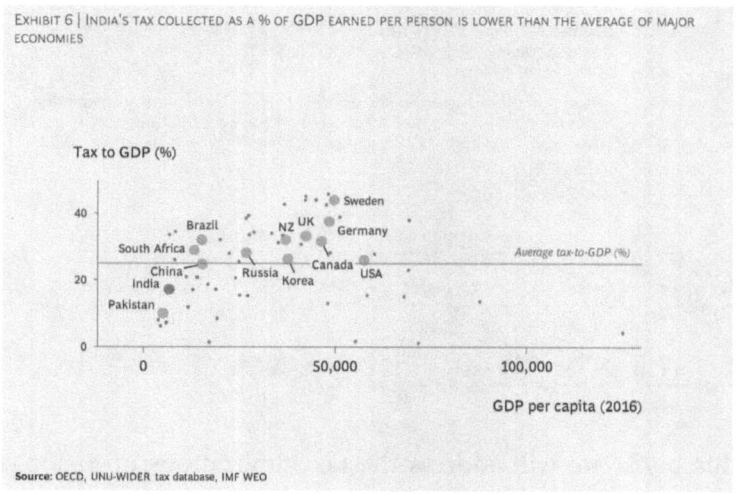

Total tax collected is a function of direct and indirect tax collections. Direct tax collections depend on the taxpayer net, or the total people filing taxes, and average tax filed per person. On the other hand, Indirect tax collections depend on the willingness of people to pay taxes honestly and comply with laws as well as how easy the system makes it to comply with these laws (Exhibit 7).

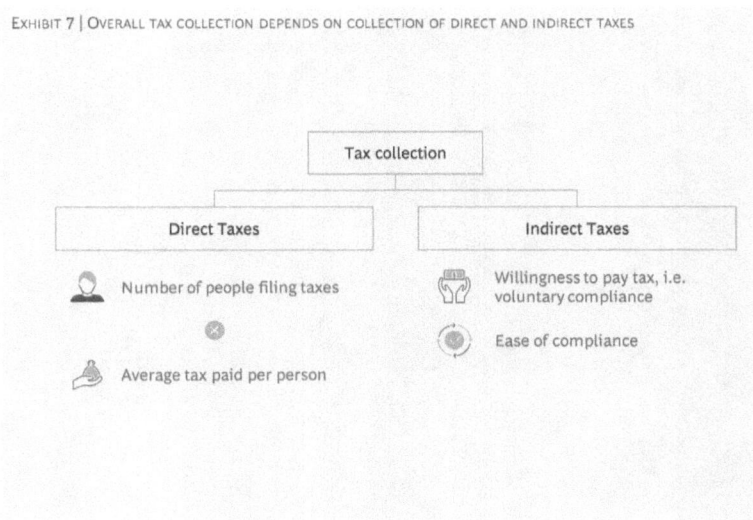

EXHIBIT 7 | OVERALL TAX COLLECTION DEPENDS ON COLLECTION OF DIRECT AND INDIRECT TAXES

In terms of direct tax collections, India's tax base has been consistently growing due to the efforts of the government in increasing the number of taxpayers (Exhibit 8).

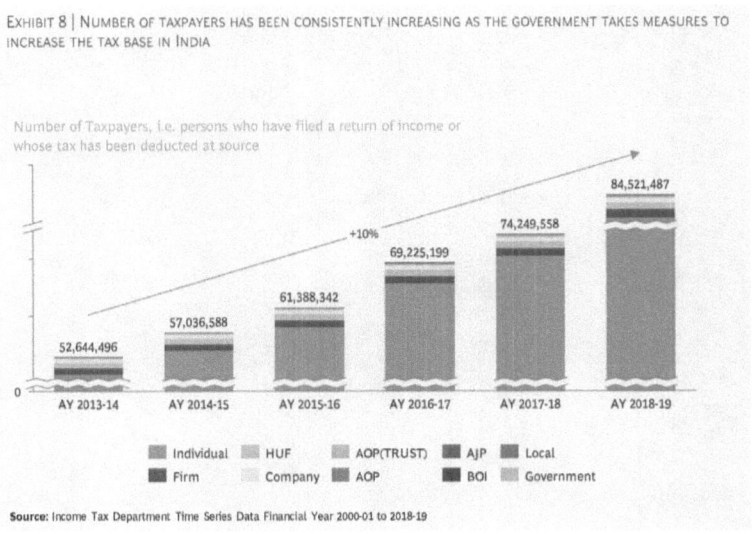

EXHIBIT 8 | NUMBER OF TAXPAYERS HAS BEEN CONSISTENTLY INCREASING AS THE GOVERNMENT TAKES MEASURES TO INCREASE THE TAX BASE IN INDIA

Source: Income Tax Department Time Series Data Financial Year 2000-01 to 2018-19

However, we have a long way to go in widening the tax net when we compare ourselves to other economies like US, UK, Japan, Brazil or China, where 10-50% of the population pays taxes (Exhibit 9).

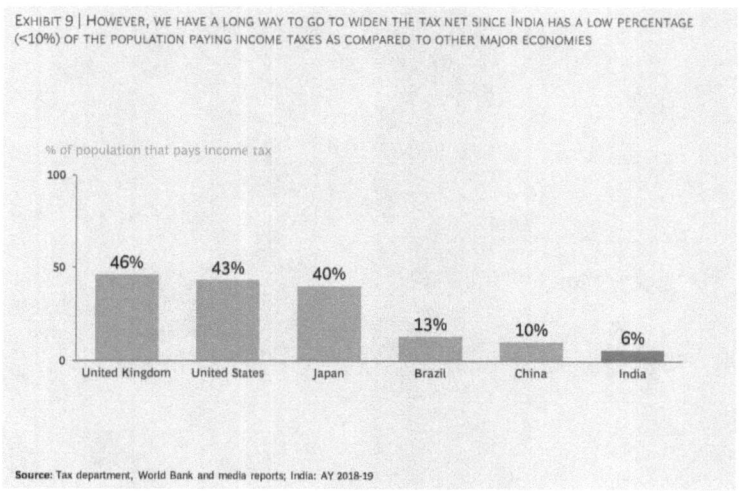

EXHIBIT 9 | HOWEVER, WE HAVE A LONG WAY TO GO TO WIDEN THE TAX NET SINCE INDIA HAS A LOW PERCENTAGE (<10%) OF THE POPULATION PAYING INCOME TAXES AS COMPARED TO OTHER MAJOR ECONOMIES

Moreover, out of the total returns filed, >2 crore returns were filed with zero income tax liability. This is an indication of the low levels of average income tax paid by individuals in the country (Exhibit 10).

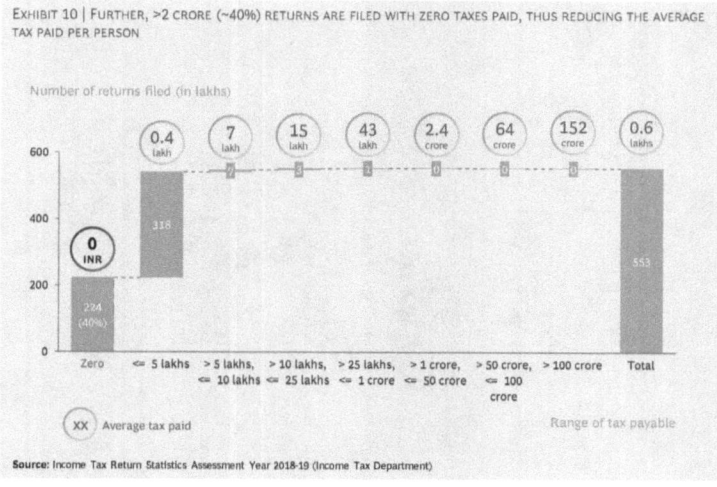

EXHIBIT 10 | FURTHER, >2 CRORE (~40%) RETURNS ARE FILED WITH ZERO TAXES PAID, THUS REDUCING THE AVERAGE TAX PAID PER PERSON

As a result, the tax burden falls on select few individuals and companies since the biggest contribution to individual income tax revenue (~80%) for AY 2018-19 came from top 6% individuals and largest 4% firms contributed over 95% of the total corporate tax collections (Exhibit 11). The skewness in both income and corporate tax collections could partly reflect income inequality. But, despite the government's numerous efforts to improve the tax base, they can also arise owing to exemptions, weak administration and evasion.

Note: Assessment year is the year immediately following the financial year, example for FY 2018-19, the assessment year is 2019-20.

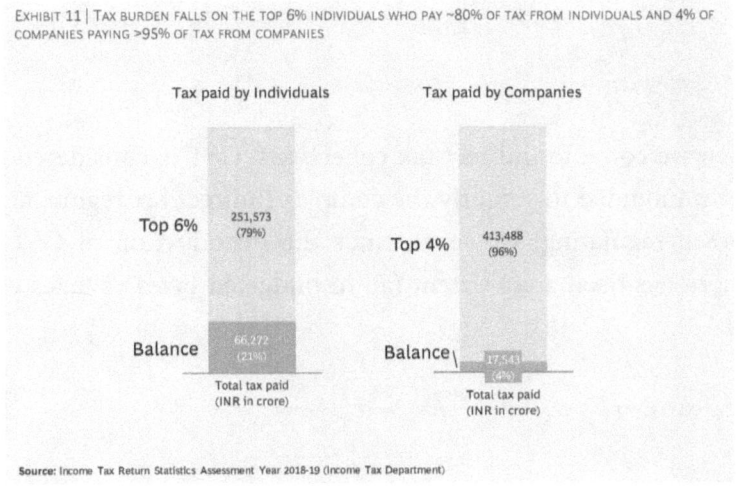

Exhibit 11 | Tax burden falls on the top 6% individuals who pay ~80% of tax from individuals and 4% of companies paying >95% of tax from companies

Source: Income Tax Return Statistics Assessment Year 2018-19 (Income Tax Department)

Within the country, states with higher per capita income levels, i.e. Maharashtra and Delhi have a lead in tax collection (Exhibit 12).

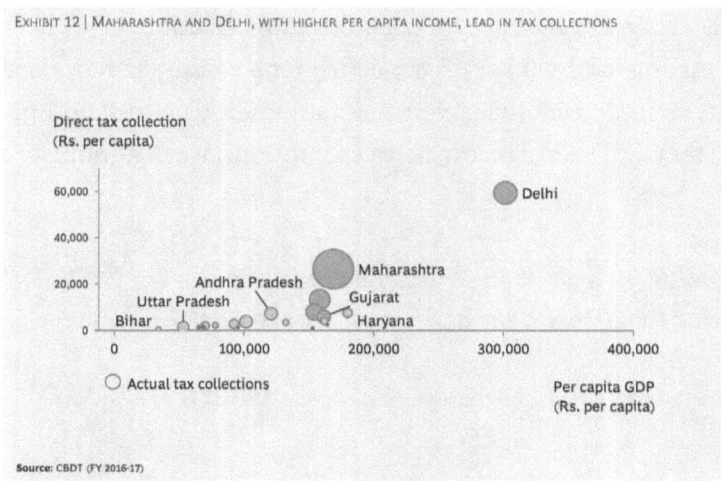

When we come to indirect tax collections, GST is considered a major tax reform intended to simplify the complex indirect tax regime and make it more self-regulating. However, since the introduction of GST in July 2017, there has been a consistent fall in budgeted taxes vs taxes collected (Exhibit 13).

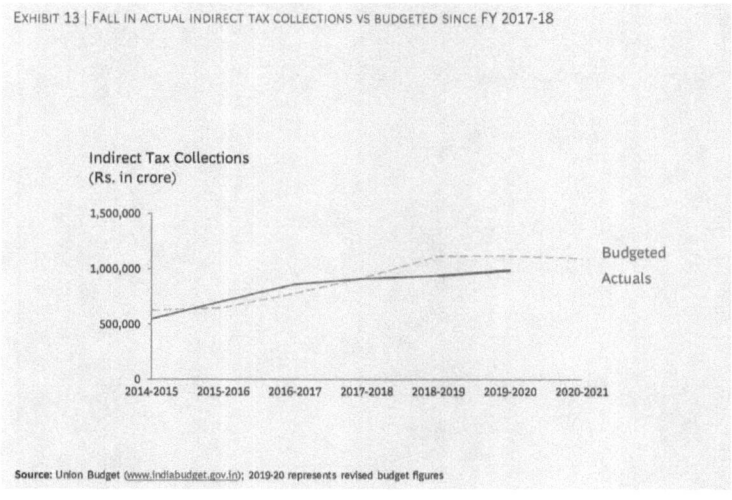

The Comptroller and Auditor General of India ('CAG') carried out an audit in 2019 calling the GST tax compliance system 'non-functional' due to complexities in the returns process and technical glitches that expose the system to fraud. Given the magnitude of the tax reform that GST has been, transiting to this system and realizing its full potential may take its course.

Tax avoidance vs tax evasion

We came across the point on 'voluntary compliance' while discussing both direct and indirect taxes above. Voluntary compliance is when taxes are paid honestly and not 'evaded'. It is here that we must understand the difference between tax avoidance and tax evasion. 'Tax avoidance' is the use of legally available tools at our disposal, such as income exemptions, deductions, etc. to reduce our tax liability. Tax evasion, on the other hand, is illegally avoiding taxes.

> *"The difference between tax avoidance and tax evasion is the thickness of a prison wall."*
>
> – Denis Healy,
> former UK Chancellor of the Exchequer

It might be easy to think that one person evading taxes will not impact the economy by a large factor. But it's also a true story that little drops make the mighty ocean. Ultimately, the taxes we pay are necessary for national development and welfare, in the absence of which, the economy as we know it ceases to function well. It doesn't mean that we cannot avoid taxes by using the tools given to us. This book is an attempt to help you navigate the complexities of taxation in India, identify the opportunities to save your money and avoid paying penalties whilst doing the same!

Demystifying Tax for the Common Man

1.6 Key takeaways

EXHIBIT 14 | KEY TAKEAWAYS FROM CHAPTER 1

 Understanding the 'What, Why and How?' of taxation can go a long way in **removing the fear in our minds about tax**, an integral part of our daily lives

 The govt. allocates its expenditure budget to debt servicing (~23%), economic development (~19%), community & social development (~17%), peace & security (~17%), general public services (~17%), etc. **~54%** of these expenditures are funded through tax revenue[1]

 Tax revenue is split into **direct tax (~54%)**[2], where burden of tax cannot be shifted to another person, e.g. income tax, & **indirect tax (~46%)**[2] where it can be passed on to the consumer, e.g. GST

 India has a relatively low tax-to-GDP ratio (~17%) vis-à-vis major economies despite the govt's efforts to increase the tax base and improve indirect tax collections

 While only **~6%** of the population pays income tax, tax burden falls on **top 6% of individuals** who pay **~79%** tax from individuals and **4% of companies** paying **~96%** tax from companies

1. Percentage of total budget (FY 2020-21); 2. Percentage of budgeted gross tax revenue (INR 24.23 lakh crore in FY 2020-21)

CHAPTER 2

ORGANIZATION OF THE TAX SYSTEM IN INDIA

2.1 Introduction

In the previous chapter, we saw why taxes are levied and how the Central and State governments have the power to collect taxes, given to them by the Constitution of India. But even though the governments use taxpayers' funds for their various schemes and other expenditures, they don't directly collect taxes from you. They have established specific bodies who oversee tax administration – these are the folks you end up being in direct contact with. Let's understand more about your gateway to the tax world in this chapter.

2.2 Know your tax authorities

The government has delegated the administration of all taxes to the Central Board of Direct Taxes (CBDT) and Central Board of Indirect Taxes & Customs (CBIC) (Exhibit 15).

EXHIBIT 15 | TAX ADMINISTRATION IN INDIA

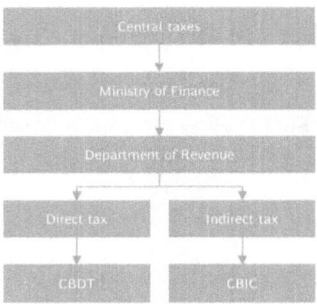

The CBDT administers actual collection of direct taxes through the Income Tax department. In case of indirect taxes, these are only collected at the time of making purchases. Thus, the authorities need not worry about their collection per se. However, there are still authorities in-charge of ensuring proper tax collections.

2.3 Your tax authorities have a hierarchy too

2.3.1 Direct tax authorities

The CBDT has a hierarchy of tax authorities under its power (Exhibit 16).

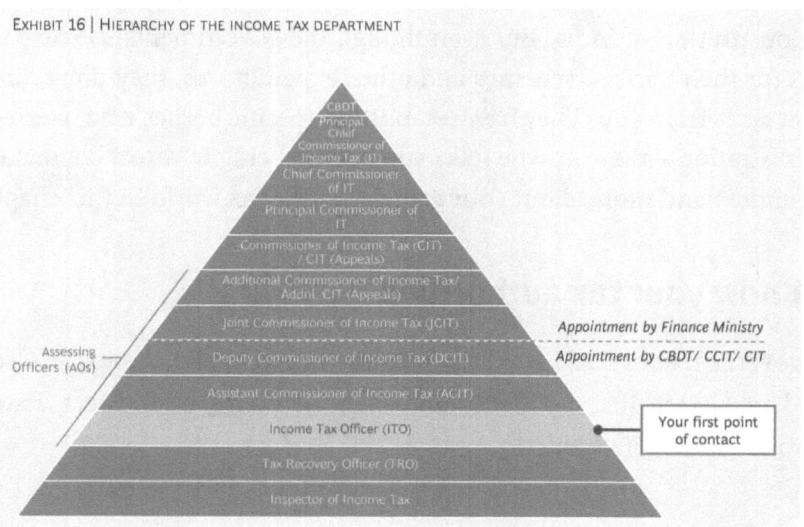

In the grand scheme of things, we – the Mango people, or Aam Aadmi, are called 'Assessees'. Assessees are any persons whose incomes are 'assessed' and who are supposed to pay taxes on such incomes. It doesn't have to be a living individual; it can be any 'person'. An assessee can be you, your employer (the company), or your family business (a sole proprietorship or partnership firm), etc.

As an assessee, your first point of contact is usually the Income Tax Officer, i.e. the person who might reach out to you by sending an 'Income

Tax notice'. Refer Chapter 6 on tax compliances to know more about kinds of notices and how to reply to them.

Apart from the above, there are many other sections/ departments in the income tax authority dealing with income tax matters.

2.3.2 Indirect tax authorities

On the indirect tax front, the CBIC is responsible for:

1. Forming collection policies for GST (Central and Integrated), Customs duty, Central Excise duty, prevention of smuggling; and

2. Administration of GST (Central and Integrated), Customs duty, Central Excise duty and Narcotics

In this chapter, we are getting into the hierarchy of the most popular indirect tax, GST's authorities (Exhibit 17). The GST Council is solely responsible for any revision or rule or any rate changes of the goods and services in India. On the other hand, the GST Department under the CBIC is in-charge of administration of GST.

EXHIBIT 17 | HIERARCHY OF GST AUTHORITIES

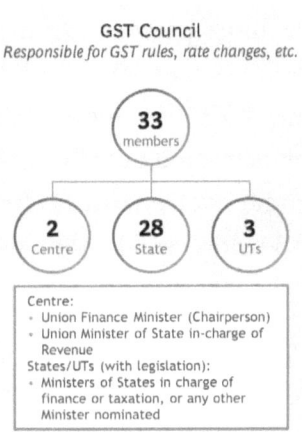
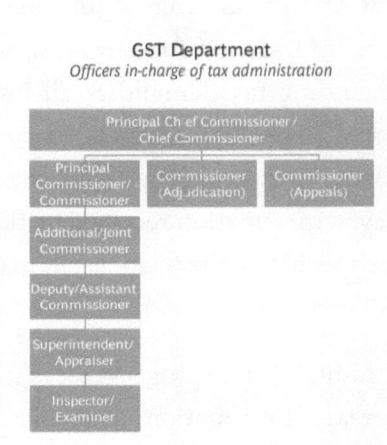

2.4 Ensuring your honesty – information sources used by the IT department

The tax departments want to ensure that people do not evade taxes. To do this, they have several sources of information at their disposal, including:

1. TDS returns (Form 26AS)
2. Transactions where your Permanent Account Number (PAN) is quoted
3. Statement of Financial Transactions (SFT) from third parties such as banks, credit card companies, mutual funds, etc.
4. Project Insight – an insight into your life

1. TDS returns (Form 26AS)

It is mandatory to furnish PAN for all transactions where tax is to be deducted at source. These details are annually recorded in 'Form 26AS' for an assessee. You can access your Form 26AS from the Income Tax website and use the same for filing your tax returns since it provides details of all taxes deducted or collected at source.

However, with effect from AY 2020-21, CBDT has revamped the Form 26AS into an 'Annual Information Statement', which will provide a lot more information for assessees, such as more personal details, details of outstanding tax demand & all income tax proceedings (pending and completed), specified financial transactions (SFT) beyond certain limits (e.g. share purchase, property purchase, deposits, credit card transactions). Thus, even information received by the Income Tax Department from filers of these specified SFTs (elaborated in point 3 below) will be shown in Form 26AS.

In addition to helping assessees file ITRs, this will assist tax authorities to compare information available in Form 26AS with ITRs during e-assessments and flag any mismatch without much interaction with assessees.

2. Transactions with PAN

It is compulsory for your PAN to be quoted on certain transactions (Exhibit 18). Hence, every such high-value transaction can be tracked by the department in case it is not disclosed in the tax returns.

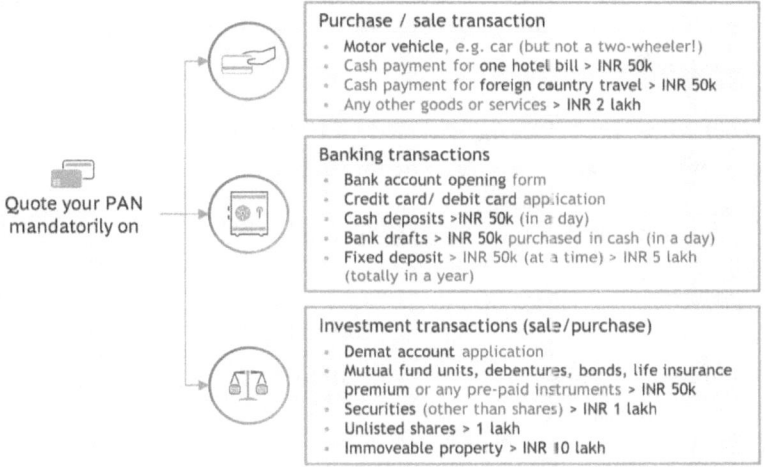

EXHIBIT 18 | THERE ARE CERTAIN PURCHASE/SALE, BANKING AND INVESTMENT TRANSACTIONS ON WHICH QUOTING YOUR PAN IS MANDATORY

Quote your PAN mandatorily on

Purchase / sale transaction
- Motor vehicle, e.g. car (but not a two-wheeler!)
- Cash payment for one hotel bill > INR 50k
- Cash payment for foreign country travel > INR 50k
- Any other goods or services > INR 2 lakh

Banking transactions
- Bank account opening form
- Credit card/ debit card application
- Cash deposits >INR 50k (in a day)
- Bank drafts > INR 50k purchased in cash (in a day)
- Fixed deposit > INR 50k (at a time) > INR 5 lakh (totally in a year)

Investment transactions (sale/purchase)
- Demat account application
- Mutual fund units, debentures, bonds, life insurance premium or any pre-paid instruments > INR 50k
- Securities (other than shares) > INR 1 lakh
- Unlisted shares > 1 lakh
- Immoveable property > INR 10 lakh

3. Third-party reporting entities

SFT is a report of specified financial transactions by specified persons who register, maintain or record such transactions to submit to the Income Tax authority. E.g. any high-value transaction you do with your bank(s), credit cards, brokers/mutual funds above a specified threshold get reported.

Sl. No	Nature of transaction to be reported	Monetary threshold of transaction	Specified person required to submit SFT
1	Cash purchase of bank drafts or pay orders or banker's cheque	Aggregating to Rs 10 lakh or more in a FY	Bank
	Cash purchase of pre-paid instruments issued by RBI	Aggregating to Rs 10 lakh or more in a FY	
	Cash deposits in current account	Aggregating to Rs 50 lakh or more in a FY	
	Cash withdrawals from current	Aggregating to Rs 50 lakh or more in a FY	
2	Cash deposits in accounts other than a current account or time deposit	Aggregating to Rs 10 lakh or more in a FY	Bank
3	Time deposits	Aggregating to Rs 10 lakh or more in a FY	Bank/NBFC
4	Credit card payments in a FY	Aggregating to Rs 1 lakh or more in cash or Rs 10 lakh or more by any other mode in a FY	Bank/other credit card company
5	Receipt for new bonds or debentures	Aggregating to Rs 10 lakh or more in a FY	Issuer
6	Receipt for shares	Aggregating to Rs 10 lakh or more in a FY	Issuer
7	Buyback of shares (not from open market)	Aggregating to Rs 10 lakh or more in a FY	Listed company
8	Receipt for new mutual fund units	Aggregating to Rs 10 lakh or more in a FY	Mutual Fund manager

Sl. No	Nature of transaction to be reported	Monetary threshold of transaction	Specified person required to submit SFT
9	Receipt for foreign currency	Aggregating to Rs 10 lakh or more during a FY	Authorised persons
10	Purchase or sale of immovable property	Rs 30 lakhs or more	Registrar
11	Cash receipt for any other goods or services of any nature	Exceeding Rs 2 lakh	Any person who is liable for audit under section 44AB of the Act

The department uses technology, data analysis and artificial intelligence to comb through these large transactions and track people who do not file their returns despite entering into many such high-value transactions. Hence, if such transactions are being reported in your bank accounts, they should be properly reported.

4. Project Insight – an insight into your life

Next time you go on a vacation and think of uploading a vacation album or #ThrowbackThursday post on Facebook or Instagram, do keep in mind that these might be getting tracked.

The Income Tax department has a business intelligence platform, or simply tracker, called 'Project Insight', developed at a cost of ~1,000 crore. This will scout the vast pool of data of social networking sites and create a 360-degree profile of taxpayers. Not just social media, even data available with other government bodies – such as GST database, Registrar of Companies (where you register a new company), RBI records, etc. may be shared and used to find any taxpayers who may be high risk tax evaders.

Hence, disclosures across different aspects of your life must speak to each other and be in line. For instance, if your 'Input Tax Credit' claims or turnover details for GST don't match with your personal tax records, then questions can be asked.

There are two new centers set up to facilitate this –

a. **Income Tax Transaction Analysis Centre (INTRAC)**: for data mining, integration from different sources, processing and quality monitoring to ultimately leverage data analytics in tax administration

b. **Compliance Management Centralized Processing Centre (CMCPC)**: to support voluntary compliance by sending out emails, SMS, reminders, outbound calls, letters and resolving any compliance issues without physical interaction

Officials will be able to spot those who pay too little tax without harassing assessees by raiding homes or offices. This will also bring an end to any randomness in scrutiny. World over countries like Belgium, Canada and Australia already use big data to curb tax evasion. India is heading towards a threefold goal through Project Insight - to bring more people under the tax net, catch citizens who avoid paying tax and bring an end to existing violation cases with pending tax demands.

2.5 Consultants to the government – TPRU and TPC

Back in 2016, the government relied on two separate bodies for handling tax policies – Tax Research Unit for indirect taxes and Tax Policy and Legislation for direct taxes. However, based on suggestions of the Tax Administration Reform Commission (TARC), the government updated their institutions to keep one consistent Tax Policy Council (TPC), supported by a common Tax Policy Research Unit (TPRU) for catering to both, direct and indirect taxes.

The roles of these institutions are critical since they advise the government on important matters that ultimately affect us all.

Tax Policy Research Unit (TPRU)

The TPRU's role is to:

- ❖ Conduct studies on tax and fiscal policies referred to it by CBDT and CBEC and offer their independent analysis
- ❖ Prepare and distribute policy papers and background papers on different tax policy issues (unfortunately, these are not available in the public domain)
- ❖ Assist TPC in taking tax policy decisions
- ❖ Liaise with the commercial tax departments of states

The TPRU's scope includes changes in the tax rates as well – e.g. while determining the recent tax rate cuts for companies, TPRU's research into turnover of companies and the effective corporate tax rate borne by them was leveraged. Accordingly, impact on government's total tax collection, after considering decrease in tax rates, partially offset by increase in tax compliance, is calculated.

While conducting their research and giving recommendations, the TPRU must be careful of the following important aspects:

1. Why the proposal is being framed and objective of the policy (as lawyers call it 'legislative intent')
2. Expected decrease or increase in tax collection as a result of the proposal
3. Expected economic impact of the proposal other than on tax collection

Thus, the TPRU consists of officers from both, CBDT and CBEC, statisticians, economists, legal experts and operational researchers.

Tax Policy Council (TPC)

EXHIBIT 19 | TAX POLICY COUNCIL (TPC)

Structure of TPC

1. Finance Minister – Chairperson
2. Minister of State for Finance
3. Deputy Chairman, NITI Aayog
4. Minister of State for Commerce & Industry
5. Finance Secretary
6. Secretary, Department of Economic Affairs
7. Revenue Secretary
8. Secretary, Commerce
9. Secretary, DIPP
10. Chief Economic Advisor to the Finance Minister

Functions of TPC

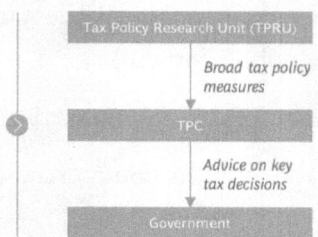

2.6 Key takeaways

EXHIBIT 20 | KEY TAKEAWAYS FROM CHAPTER 2

CBDT and CBIC handle collection of direct and indirect taxes in India respectively

From a direct tax perspective, your first point of contact will generally be the **Income Tax Officer of your jurisdiction**

You must **quote your PAN card** on specified purchase/sale, banking & investment transactions over certain limits

The Income Tax Department uses many tools to ensure that you pay your taxes honestly - it has access to your **TDS returns, PAN-transactions, banking details** & software leveraging other data sources, e.g. GST database, RBI records, RoC, even social media accounts!

These tools are enablers for the Income Tax Department to spot tax avoiders scientifically, end violations and bring more people under tax net

The government has also put in place bodies (TPRU and TPC) which assist them in **forming consistent tax policies** across direct and indirect taxes

• CHAPTER 3 •

ELEMENTAL TAX KNOWLEDGE FOR A SALARIED PERSON

3.1 Introduction

In the first chapter, we covered how the tax burden falls on 'persons', and how that doesn't just mean a living, breathing individual. However, since we are covering the major taxes on individuals and businesses / professions in this book, let's begin with the first – taxes paid by you and me (i.e. if you too are working for someone else). For an individual working a job, their 'salary' would be the main income source, and they would be regularly paying taxes to the government on this. Let's see what exactly salary means, how it is taxed, what portion of the salary one ends up paying as tax and how to reduce the tax burden.

3.2 What does my 'salary' include?

Salary is simple, right? You work 25 days in a month and get paid for it by end of the month. But as always, the Income Tax Act has rules that need to be followed. Just because money is called salary doesn't mean that it is. For any payment to be called 'salary', the person receiving it must be an employee of the person paying it.

In simple terms, if you have your own business and draw a 'salary' from this business for your blood, sweat and tears, it won't be taxed as salary but as 'Profits and gains of business and profession'. It also doesn't matter if you have left your job and joined another organization in a year – the salary from your ex-employer will still be called salary and will be taxed the same way that year.

To the taxman, salary doesn't just mean the fixed monthly remuneration you receive from your employer. The Income Tax Act has defined 'salary' to include many things, whether received in cash or in kind:

- ❖ Basic salary, fees, commission and bonus
- ❖ Allowances, such as dearness allowance (DA), allowance for house rent, children education, etc.
- ❖ Perquisites, or 'perks', such as rent-free accommodation, use of motor car or any other obligation discharged by the employer
- ❖ Retirement benefits, such as gratuity, pension, provident fund, voluntary retirement compensation
- ❖ Other items: Leave salary encashment, leave travel concession, retrenchment compensation

Adding all the above items brings us to a figure called 'gross salary' (Exhibit 21). The final income to be taxed as salary, however, is arrived at after reducing certain items allowed as 'deductions' from salary (Exhibit 22). These include:

- ❖ Standard deduction
- ❖ Entertainment allowance (only if you're a government employee)
- ❖ Professional tax paid

This salary amount is added to other incomes to calculate total taxable income.

EXHIBIT 21 | GROSS SALARY MAINLY COMPRISES BASIC SALARY, ALLOWANCES, PERQUISITES AND RETIREMENT BENEFITS

Gross salary

- **Basic salary:** The actual pay you receive for your services
- **Bonus or commission:** Variable pay as per company policy

- **Allowances**
  - Dearness allowance: to compensate the rising cost of living in your location
  - House Rent allowance: to meet your house rent
  - Conveyance allowance: to cover the commute expenses between your home to work
  - Leave Travel allowance: to cover domestic travel expenses, excluding food, stay, etc.
  - Others: Special allowance, medical allowance, children education, etc.

- **Perquisites**
  - Rent free accommodation: House provided by employer for staying
  - Use of motor car: Expenses by the employer on a car used by employee
  - Others: any obligation of employee borne by employer

- **Retirement benefits**
  - Gratuity: Retirement benefit which can be availed after completing 5 years on the job
  - Pension: Regular payment received post retirement from fund collected during service
  - Provident Fund: Investment fund from which lump sum is received post retirement

- **Other items**
  - Leave salary encashment: Money paid for leaves not utilized during the work term
  - Retrenchment compensation: Any amount paid on being terminated (non-disciplinary)

EXHIBIT 22 | TAXABLE (OR NET) SALARY IS GROSS SALARY REDUCED BY CERTAIN ALLOWABLE DEDUCTIONS

Gross salary

Deductions

- **Standard deduction:** ₹ 50,000 flat deduction from total salary income

- **Profession tax:** Tax on employment levied by a state (up to ₹ 2,500), usually deducted by the employer and allowed as a deduction from salary income

- **Entertainment allowance:** Deductible only if you're a government employee! This is offered to employees for any expenses on customer hospitality

Taxable salary

3.3 How is my salary taxed?

You might remember how your monthly salary amount multiplied by 12 seemed less than what you imagined your annual salary would be the first time. This is because what you are told initially is the 'CTC' or 'Cost-to-Company', and what you ultimately receive is the 'take-home' or in-hand salary.

CTC is the total cost of employing you to your employer – basic salary, HRA, allowances, provident fund, pension fund, any incentives paid, etc. Basically, all direct, indirect incomes and savings contributions are added to form the CTC. But you don't receive all these every 30th/31st of the month. The employer reduces things like your income tax, provident fund contribution, profession tax, etc. and pays you the balance amount (sample pay slip below).

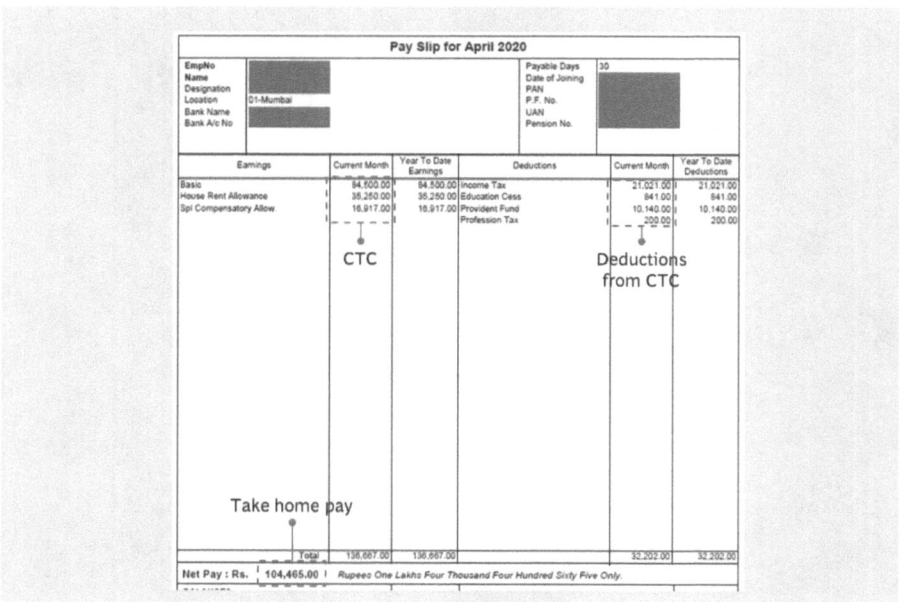

This is also where we'd like to highlight the concept of 'tax deducted at source' or TDS.

So that you, the taxpayer, don't have to worry about extra compliance with paying taxes, the government levies TDS on a list of incomes. Salary paid by an employer is one such income, where it is the responsibility of the employer to pay out monthly salary after reducing the monthly tax payable.

In order to know how much tax needs to be deducted, the employer asks for details of your other incomes and investments to compute annual tax payable by you. This amount is divided by 12 and reduced from your monthly salary to calculate salary 'in-hand'.

3.4 What is the rate at which my salary is taxed?

All incomes derived by an individual, including salary income, are taxed in a 'progressive' way. This means that as you earn higher incomes, you pay a higher tax rate on those. Moreover, the rates of tax for respective income levels change as you become older!

Up until 1 February 2020, there existed only one regime of taxation for individuals. Under this regime, individuals were provided relief in the form of deductions from their income and exemptions on certain types of incomes. However, to move to a simplified tax system, revised income slabs and lower tax rates thereon were introduced (Exhibit 23).

This new regime has been kept optional, to be exercised every year, if the individual does not have business income. In case the individual has business income, option once exercised will be applicable for all future years with a one-time option to change, except where such person ceases to have business income. The catch is that taxpayers can opt for the 'new regime' only if they let go of several exemptions, deductions and their option to set off certain losses from other incomes.

EXHIBIT 23 | INCOME SLABS AND TAX RATES FOR INDIVIDUALS UNDER OLD REGIME AND NEW REGIME WITH EFFECT FROM 1 APRIL 2021

Individuals less than 60 years old			Individuals from 60 - 80 years old			Individuals more than 80 years old		
Income slab	Old regime	New regime	Income slab	Old regime	New regime	Income slab	Old regime	New regime
0 – 2.5 lakhs	Exempt	Exempt	0 – 3 lakhs	Exempt	Exempt	0 – 5 lakhs	Exempt	Exempt
2.5 – 5 lakhs¹	5%	5%	3 – 5 lakhs¹	5%	5%	5 – 7.5 lakhs	20%	10%
5 – 7.5 lakhs	20%	10%	5 – 7.5 lakhs	20%	10%	7.5 – 10 lakhs		15%
7.5 – 10 lakhs		15%	7.5 – 10 lakhs		15%	10 – 12.5 lakhs		20%
10 – 12.5 lakhs		20%	10 – 12.5 lakhs		20%	12.5 – 15 lakhs	30%	25%
12.5 – 15 lakhs	30%	25%	12.5 – 15 lakhs	30%	25%	Above 15 lakhs		30%
Above 15 lakhs		30%	Above 15 lakhs		30%			

1. Individuals with yearly taxable income up to Rs 5 lakhs will get full tax rebate under section 87A
2. Note: The above doesn't include cess or surcharge

Source: Finance Bill, 2020

Going forward, let's work with the example of individuals less than 60 years old for calculation purposes.

3.5 How can I reduce the tax incidence on my salary income?

There are typically three avenues to reduce tax incidence on salaried income:

1. Allowances exempt as part of salary
2. Deductions from salary
3. Losses from other incomes set-off against salary

Given that majority of the above avenues are not available under the new regime, let us look at the two regimes separately to understand how to reduce the tax incidence on salary.

Under the old regime

There is a long list of allowances, and an even longer list of how to claim exemptions from such allowances. But, as salaried individuals, there are a select few allowances which one can consider common for all and exemptions from there are key in reducing your taxable salary. Let us look at those in detail (Exhibits 24 and 25). We have also provided the laundry list of other allowances and exemptions you may come across.

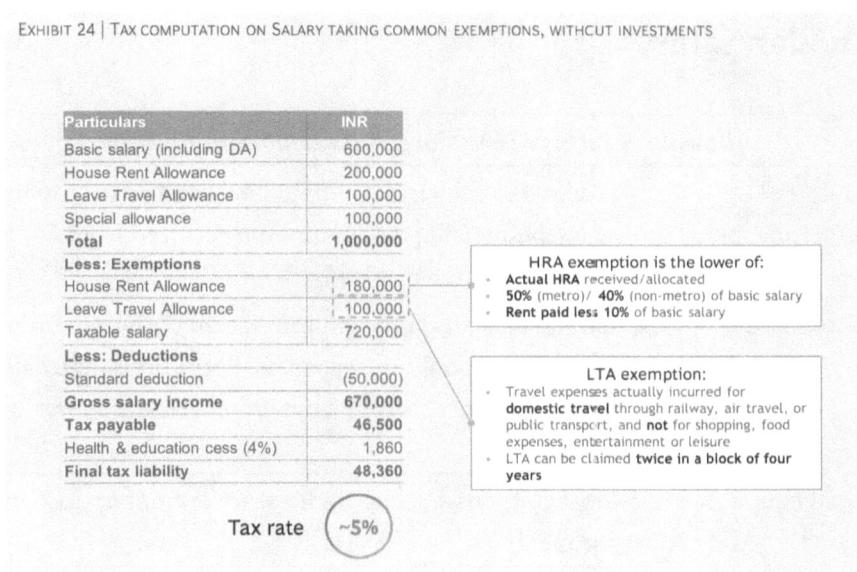

Exhibit 24 | Tax computation on Salary taking common exemptions, without investments

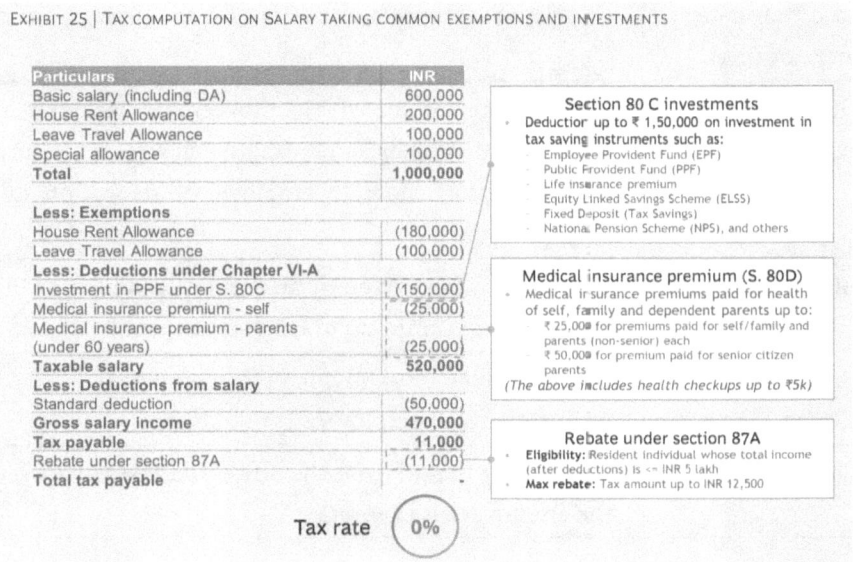

Exhibit 25 | Tax computation on Salary taking common exemptions and investments

See how you can significantly reduce your tax burden using exemptions on allowances and investments? Like we promised, a non-exhaustive list of other exemptions and deductions is given below:

1. Other exemptions from certain incomes included under 'salary'

Allowances included in salary and exemptions thereon	
Mobile reimbursement	Employees can claim reimbursement of actual mobile or telephone bill paid, or amount received from employer, whichever is lower
Books and periodicals	Employees can claim reimbursement of the expenses incurred on books, newspapers, periodicals, journals, etc. or amount received from employer, whichever is lower
Food coupons	Meal coupons, such as Sodexo, are exempt up to ₹ 50 per meal
Initial accommodation on relocation	Accommodation provided by employer on relocation (boarding and meals) is exempt for the initial 15 days
Other relocation expenses	Car transportation cost (e.g. movers and packers), car registration charges, packaging charges and train or air tickets provided by employer on relocation are exempt
Gifts or vouchers	Gifts or vouchers given by an employer in cash or in kind are tax exempt up to ₹ 5,000 per year
Health club facility	Health club facility provided by an employer uniformly to all employees is not taxable
Cab facility	Cab facility to and from the office and residence of the employees is exempt

Medical expenditure incurred outside India	Expenditure on medical treatment of employees or their family is exempt to the extent permitted by the Reserve Bank of India, for employees whose gross total income does not exceed ₹ 2,00,000
Retirement benefits	
Gratuity	In case of government employees, gratuity received on retirement or death is fully exempt
	For other employees, exemption depends on whether the employer is covered by the Payment of Gratuity Act (POGA):
	If covered by POGA, least of the following is exempt:
	− (Last drawn Basic Salary +DA)*(15/26)*(Number of years in employment rounded off to nearest full year)
	− ₹ 20,00,000
	− Gratuity actually received
	If not covered by POGA, least of the following is exempt
	− (Average monthly salary of last 10 months)*(1/2)*(Number of completed years in employment)
	− ₹ 20,00,000
	− Gratuity actually received
	This exemption is cumulative of all gratuity payments received by an individual in his/her lifetime

Pension	Pension received periodically is fully taxable. However, exemptions exist in case of commuted, or lump sum pension:
	
	– For government employees: Fully exempt
	
	– For other employees:
	
	   o If gratuity is received, up to 1/3rd of total pension
	
	   o If gratuity is not received, up to 1/2 of total pension

Leave salary encashment	It is fully exempt for government employees. For other employees, least of the following is exempt: – 10 months average salary (basic + DA) before retirement – Leave encashment actually received – ₹ 3,00,000
Voluntary retirement scheme	Least of the following is exempt once in the life-time of an employee: – Amount actually received – ₹ 5,00,000 – Amount calculated as per guidelines of scheme, i.e. lower of (three months' salary)*(completed years of service) or actual salary for balance months of service
Employer contribution to Provident Fund, etc.	From 1 April 2020, total employer contribution to provident fund, superannuation fund or National Pension Scheme > ₹ 7,50,000 is taxable Thus, any interest, dividend, etc. related to the taxable amount is also taxable

2. Deductions from salary and total income

Deductions from salary	
Standard deduction	Flat ₹ 50,000 deduction from the total income
Entertainment allowance	Deduction for such allowance is available only to government employees, as least of the following: – Amount actually received – 1/5th of basic salary – ₹ 5,000
Professional tax	Professional tax, whether paid by employer or employee, is fully allowed as a deduction without any limit
Other major deductions from total income	
Section 80C, 80CCC, 80CCD(1) [Longer list]	Deduction up to ₹ 1,50,000 on investment in tax saving instruments, such as: – Life insurance premium – Equity Linked Savings Scheme (ELSS) – Employee Provident Fund (EPF) – Public Provident Fund (PPF) – Annuity/ Pension Schemes – Principal payment on home loans – Tuition fees for children – Sukanya Samriddhi Account – NSC (National Saving Certificate) – Fixed Deposit (Tax Savings) – Post office time deposits – National Pension Scheme (NPS)

Section 80CCD(1B)	Additional deduction up to ₹ 50,000 can be claimed for self-contribution to NPS
Interest on home loan	Up to ₹2,00,000 can be claimed as deduction on interest paid on home loans, provided acquisition or construction of the house is completed within 5 years from end of financial year of availing the loan
	Further, housing loan repayment can be claimed as a deduction under 80C up to ₹ 1,50,000
Interest on home loan (Additional deduction – 80EE and 80EEA)	Additional deduction of interest on home loan up to ₹50,000 provided the loan amount is up to ₹35,00,000 and the value of the property is up to ₹50,00,000
	For first time home buyers not entitled to the above, interest deduction up to ₹1,50,000 is permitted for affordable housing loan taken up to 31 March 2021 (where property value does not exceed ₹45,00,000)
Loan for higher studies	Interest on loan taken from a bank or a financial institution for pursuing higher studies (in India or abroad) can be availed without any limit up to 8 years
Donations	This deduction varies based on the receiving organization from 50% or 100% of the amount donated, with or without restriction
Savings account interest	Up to ₹ 10,000 can be claimed as interest on savings account with a bank or post office. In case of senior citizens, the limit is enhanced to ₹ 50,000.
Disability	Up to ₹ 75,000 (₹1,25,000 in case of severe disability) as disability-related benefits for self, dependent spouse, child, parent or even sibling.
Specified diseases	Up to ₹ 40,000 (₹ 1,00,000 for patients who are 60 years or more) as treatment for certain diseases, such as AIDS or malignant cancer, for self and dependents.

A summary of major deductions is given below:

TDS on payment of rent by Individuals or HUF tenants (not subject to tax audit)

Individual tenants paying monthly rent on land or building exceeding Rs. 50,000 to resident landlords must also deduct tax at source (TDS) at the rate of **5%** from the rent payable and deposit the same with the government.

But the good news is the tenant does not need a Tax Deduction Account Number (TAN). The Tenant must quote his or her PAN and PAN of the landlord (TDS rate is 20% in case landlord's PAN is not available).

However, the deductor (tenant) must comply with the following:

a. Furnish information about the transaction online on the TIN website (www.tin-nsdl.com) via Form 26QC

b. Make the payment to the government online (through e-tax payment) immediately or subsequently through net banking or visiting any authorised bank branch *(the payment must be made within 30 days from end of the month in which the deduction is made)*

c. Issue TDS certificate to the deductee (landlord) under Form 16C

3. Losses from other incomes set-off against salary

Only loss from house property income can be used to reduce salary income. The same is restricted to ₹2,00,000, which is possible when the house property is used for self-occupation without receiving any rent, and interest paid on home loans is claimed as a deduction. *Note: Set-off of losses is explained in detail in Chapter 5 – Other taxes.*

Under the new regime

As mentioned earlier, individuals who choose to opt for the lower tax rates under the new regime are denied approximately 70 out of 100 deductions and exemptions; few of the major ones are mentioned below (Exhibit 26):

- Leave travel concession
- House rent allowance
- Standard deduction, professional tax and entertainment allowance deductions
- Interest on home loans
- Specified deductions for investments, expenditure and donations (under Chapter VI-A), such as investments under Section 80C,

medical insurance premium paid, savings bank interest, education loan interest, etc. barring a few

❖ Other specified exemptions, deductions, set-off of loss, etc. depending on specific cases

EXHIBIT 26 | MAJOR DEDUCTIONS/EXEMPTIONS ARE NOT AVAILABLE UNDER THE NEW TAX REGIME OPTION

Deductions / Exemptions	Old Tax Regime	New Tax Regime
HRA exemption	✓	✗
LTA exemption	✓	✗
Standard deduction of 50K	✓	✗
Sec. 24 • Interest on Housing Loan (Self Occupied) • Loss on Let-Out Property	✓ ✓	✗ ✗
Sec. 80 C deduction of INR 1.5 lacs (PF, LIC, PPF, ELSS, Fixed Deposits, Children Edu)	✓	✗
Sec. 80 D - Medical insurance	✓	✗
Sec. 80 E, 80DD, 80DDB - Interest on education loan, certain medical expenses	✓	✗
Sec. 80CCD (1B) - NPS Self Voluntary Contribution (INR 50K)	✓	✗
Sec. 80CCD (2) - NPS Corporate Contribution (up to 10% of basic salary)	✓	✓

Given the above, it becomes important to calculate the tax pay out under both old and new regimes to understand which is more beneficial.

3.6 The choice between different tax regimes

The answer to the question "Am I richer or poorer under the new regime of tax" depends on your level of income and to what extent you used tax-saving investments in the old regime. Thus, pensioners and new entrants to the job market, who have no investments in tax saving schemes or HRA and LTA benefits, may gain under the new tax regime (Exhibit 27).

EXHIBIT 27 | INDIVIDUALS WHO DON'T AVAIL EXEMPTIONS OR HAVE NO INVESTMENTS IN TAX SAVINGS SCHEMES (E.G. NEW ENTRANTS TO THE JOB MARKET), MAY GAIN UNDER THE NEW REGIME

Income	Rs. 7.5 lakhs		Rs. 12 lakhs		Rs. 15 lakhs		Rs. 18 lakhs		Rs. 30 lakhs	
Regime	Old	New	Old	New	Old	New	Old	New	Old	New
Taxable income	750,000	750,000	1,200,000	1,200,000	1,500,000	1,500,000	1,800,000	1,800,000	3,000,000	3,000,000
Exemptions	-	-	-	-	-	-	-	-	-	-
Deductions										
Standard deduction	(50,000)	-	(50,000)	-	(50,000)	-	(50,000)	-	(50,000)	-
Net taxable income	700,000	750,000	1,150,000	1,200,000	1,450,000	1,500,000	1,750,000	1,800,000	2,950,000	3,000,000
Tax payable	52,500	37,500	157,500	115,000	247,500	187,500	337,500	277,500	697,500	637,500
Cess @ 4%	2,100	1,500	6,300	4,600	9,900	7,500	13,500	11,100	27,900	25,500
Total tax payable	54,600	39,000	163,800	119,600	257,400	195,000	351,000	288,600	725,400	663,000
Incremental tax under new regime		(15,600)		(44,200)		(62,400)		(62,400)		(62,400)

Salaried taxpayers availing deductions, such as standard deduction, Section 80C, medical insurance premium and savings bank interest will find a lower tax payout under the old regime for given levels of income. However, as level of income increases, the new regime is beneficial (Exhibit 28A) unless more deductions are availed, e.g. contribution to new pension scheme, etc. (Exhibit 28B).

EXHIBIT 28A | FOR SALARIED INDIVIDUALS CLAIMING MAJOR DEDUCTIONS (BUT NOT EXEMPTIONS FROM ALLOWANCES LIKE HRA, ETC.), OLD REGIME IS BENEFICIAL FOR LOWER LEVELS OF TOTAL INCOME

Income	Rs. 7.5 lakhs		Rs. 12 lakhs		Rs. 15 lakhs		Rs. 18 lakhs		Rs. 30 lakhs	
Regime	Old	New	Old	New	Old	New	Old	New	Old	New
Taxable income	750,000	750,000	1,200,000	1,200,000	1,500,000	1,500,000	1,800,000	1,800,000	3,000,000	3,000,000
Exemptions	-	-	-	-	-	-	-	-	-	-
Deductions										
Section 80C	(150,000)	-	(150,000)	-	(150,000)	-	(150,000)	-	(150,000)	-
Medical insurance premium	(25,000)	-	(25,000)	-	(25,000)	-	(25,000)	-	(25,000)	-
Interest income (80TTB)	(10,000)	-	(10,000)	-	(10,000)	-	(10,000)	-	(10,000)	-
Standard deduction	(50,000)	-	(50,000)	-	(50,000)	-	(50,000)	-	(50,000)	-
Net taxable income	515,000	750,000	965,000	1,200,000	1,265,000	1,500,000	1,565,000	1,800,000	2,765,000	3,000,000
Tax payable	15,500	37,500	105,500	115,000	192,000	187,500	282,000	277,500	642,000	637,500
Cess @ 4%	620	1,500	4,220	4,600	7,680	7,500	11,280	11,100	25,680	25,500
Total tax payable	16,120	39,000	109,720	119,600	199,680	195,000	293,280	288,600	667,680	663,000
Incremental tax under new regime		22,880		9,880		(4,680)		(4,680)		(4,680)

EXHIBIT 28B | OLD REGIME IS BENEFICIAL FOR TAXPAYERS AVAILING DEDUCTIONS, SUCH AS STANDARD DEDUCTION, SECTION 80C, CONTRIBUTION TO NPS, MEDICAL INSURANCE PREMIUM AND SAVINGS BANK INTEREST

Income	Rs. 7.5 lakhs		Rs. 12 lakhs		Rs. 15 lakhs		Rs. 18 lakhs		Rs. 30 lakhs	
Regime	Old	New	Old	New	Old	New	Old	New	Old	New
Taxable income	750,000	750,000	1,200,000	1,200,000	1,500,000	1,500,000	1,800,000	1,800,000	3,000,000	3,000,000
Exemptions	-	-	-	-	-	-	-	-	-	-
Deductions										
Section 80C	(150,000)	-	(150,000)	-	(150,000)	-	(150,000)	-	(150,000)	-
Medical insurance premium	(25,000)	-	(25,000)	-	(25,000)	-	(25,000)	-	(25,000)	-
National pension scheme (80CCD(1B))	(50,000)	-	(50,000)	-	(50,000)	-	(50,000)	-	(50,000)	-
Interest income (80TTB)	(10,000)	-	(10,000)	-	(10,000)	-	(10,000)	-	(10,000)	-
Standard deduction	(50,000)	-	(50,000)	-	(50,000)	-	(50,000)	-	(50,000)	-
Net taxable income	465,000	750,000	915,000	1,200,000	1,215,000	1,500,000	1,515,000	1,800,000	2,715,000	3,000,000
Tax payable	10,750	37,500	95,500	115,000	177,000	187,500	267,000	277,500	627,000	637,500
Cess @ 4%	430	1,500	3,820	4,600	7,080	7,500	10,680	11,100	25,080	25,500
Total tax payable	11,180	39,000	99,320	119,600	184,080	195,000	277,680	288,600	652,080	663,000
Incremental tax under new regime		27,820		20,280		10,920		10,920		10,920

For taxpayers also availing HRA exemption, the new regime is a non-starter (Exhibit 29). Essentially, more the deductions or exemptions you have been availing, less beneficial the new regime. However, given the number of variables involved, it is best for each taxpayer to work out individually whether the new tax regime leaves them richer or poorer.

Exhibit 29 | For taxpayers also availing HRA exemption, the new regime is a non-starter

Income	Rs. 7.5 lakhs		Rs. 12 lakhs		Rs. 15 lakhs		Rs. 18 lakhs		Rs. 30 lakhs	
Regime	Old	New	Old	New	Old	New	Old	New	Old	New
Taxable income	750,000	750,000	1,200,000	1,200,000	1,500,000	1,500,000	1,800,000	1,800,000	3,000,000	3,000,000
Exemptions		-		-		-		-		-
Deductions										
Section 80C	(150,000)	-	(150,000)	-	(150,000)	-	(150,000)	-	(150,000)	-
Medical insurance premium	(25,000)	-	(25,000)	-	(25,000)	-	(25,000)	-	(25,000)	-
HRA exemption (taken as 1/3 of total income)	(250,000)	-	(400,000)	-	(500,000)	-	(600,000)	-	(1,000,000)	-
Interest income (80TTB)	(10,000)	-	(10,000)	-	(10,000)	-	(10,000)	-	(10,000)	-
Standard deduction	(50,000)	-	(50,000)	-	(50,000)	-	(50,000)	-	(50,000)	-
Net taxable income	265,000	750,000	565,000	1,200,000	765,000	1,500,000	965,000	1,800,000	1,765,000	3,000,000
Tax payable	-	37,500	25,500	115,000	65,500	187,500	105,500	277,500	342,000	637,500
Cess @ 4%	-	1,500	1,020	4,600	2,620	7,500	4,220	11,100	13,680	25,500
Total tax payable	-	39,000	26,520	119,600	68,120	195,000	109,720	288,600	355,680	663,000
Incremental tax under new regime		39,000		93,080		126,880		178,880		307,320

3.7 Key takeaways

Exhibit 30 | Key takeaways from chapter 3

Salary mainly includes basic salary, bonus, allowances, perquisites & retirement benefits. 'Income from Salary' is **taxed progressively**, i.e. pay higher rate of tax as you earn more

Monthly salary is received after deducting a percentage of tax ('TDS'). Due to this deduction, and a few others, your **'CTC' and take-home or in-hand salary will always be different**

Salaried employees have a **choice of availing one of two regimes** to be taxed for FY 2019-20

Under the old regime, tax can be reduced through **exemption on allowances, standard deduction (INR 50k) & other deductions** via investments and/or expenditure (e.g. Section 80C investments - INR 1.50 lakhs, Medical insurance premium, etc.)

Under the new regime, major exemptions and deductions are withdrawn in exchange for **lower tax rates & more income slabs** (6 slabs vs 3 earlier)

Subject to your level of income, **if you avail more deductions and exemptions, the old regime is more beneficial.** Choose your regime wisely keeping in mind all variables!

◆ CHAPTER 4 ◆

ELEMENTAL TAX KNOWLEDGE FOR AN ENTREPRENEUR

4.1 Introduction

In the first chapter, we covered how 'persons' doesn't just mean natural persons like you or me. It could also include artificial persons, which have separate identities and can take decisions in their own name. We're talking of a company or firm of course.

As an entrepreneur starting out, you have enough on your plate to begin with. Once you start making some money, you will also worry about incidental things like taxation. Given it will soon be a very important part of your life, it's always good to know the basics. In this chapter, we will cover the 'Why, What and How' of both direct and indirect tax for businesses and share a few tips on common tax compliance aspects that you might come across in your daily life.

Chapter 4 | Elemental tax knowledge for an entrepreneur

| Why is business income taxed? | What does business income include? | How is business income taxed? | Treading with caution |

4.2 Why is business income taxed?

"A state in India will have more traders than perhaps a European nation. Trade is a great way to integrate people".

– Narendra Modi, Prime Minister of India

Entrepreneurship is the backbone of the Indian economy. The spectrum of who can be called an entrepreneur is wide – anybody from a hawker on the streets to an industrialist is a businessperson. Today, India boasts being home to more than 119 billionaires, which more than doubled from 55 billionaires in 2013, and is expected to increase to 163 in 2023[1]. Our silent performers, on the other hand, are the Micro, Small and Medium Enterprises (MSMEs) – we have more than 60 million MSME units in the country that contribute ~29% to India's GDP and ~48% to its exports[2]. We also have the second largest start-up base in the world, with 8,366 start-ups currently in 2020, following the United States at 65,785[3] (Yes, we have a long way to get there!).

But we are on the right track. According to a survey conducted by Global Entrepreneurship Monitor (GEM), almost 50% of the adult population sees good opportunities to start a firm in the area where they live. Moreover, 11% of the adult population is either an early-stage entrepreneur or the owner of a new business, while 7% are owners of an established business running for more than 3.5 years.

Operating a business in India is clearly an important source of income, for the nation as well as the government. However, when it comes to individual income tax, declared salary income is more than twice the size of the declared individual business income.

---

1 The Wealth Report (2019 Edition) by Knight Frank
2 MSME Ministry's FY 19 Annual Report; Economic Times
3 Startup Ranking

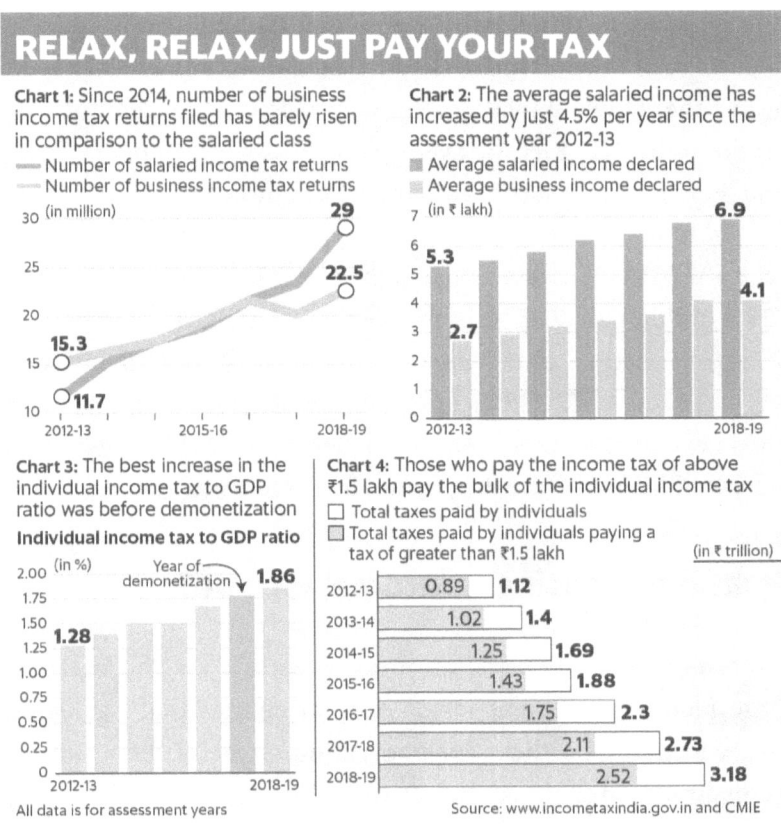

Source: Livemint

The total income declared by individuals during AY 2018-19 stood at ₹34.1 trillion. Of this ₹20 trillion, or bulk of the income, was declared by the salaried class. Business income comes in next at ₹9.3 trillion[4].

The salaried income declared jumped from ₹6.27 trillion in AY 2012-13 to ₹20 trillion in AY 2018-19, i.e. witnessed 21% CAGR. On the other hand, the business income declared during the same period has jumped from ₹4.1 trillion to ₹9.3 trillion, an increase of around 15% CAGR[5].

---

4   IT Return Statistics Assessment Year 2018-19
5   IT Return Statistics Assessment Year 2012-13

Average salary income declared in AY 2018-19 stood at ₹6.9 lakh, which is 67% more than the average declared business income of ₹4.13 lakh. This can mean either of two things: entrepreneurship is not as remunerative as it is made out to be. Or, does the average businessman still operate largely in cash and, hence, not declare their fair share of income?

Since FY 2014-15, the number of business income returns has grown from 19.4 million to 22.5 million, i.e. 5% CAGR. In comparison, the number of salaried income returns has grown from 18.9 million to 29 million, or 15% CAGR. Either businessmen are not filing returns or that many businesses have simply become unviable post 2016. It seems to be the salaried individuals who are driving the individual income tax.

4.3 What does 'business income' include?

It is important to clarify what we mean when we say, 'business income'. There are plenty of different forms of legal entities that can carry on a business, depending on their size and nature. Some of them include Sole Proprietorship, Limited Liability Partnership (LLP), Private Company, Public Company and Joint Venture. There is no legal rule that a 'Company' must be formed to start a business. If your business is growing rapidly and becomes unmanageable, it helps to separate it into a separate legal entity. Else, you may choose to carry on your business as a sole proprietor.

In this chapter, we are going to focus on business income derived by an individual, or a sole proprietor. This is included in one of the five heads of income as 'Profit and gains of Business or Profession'. Certain incomes have been defined under the Income Tax Act which are chargeable under this head of income (Exhibit 31).

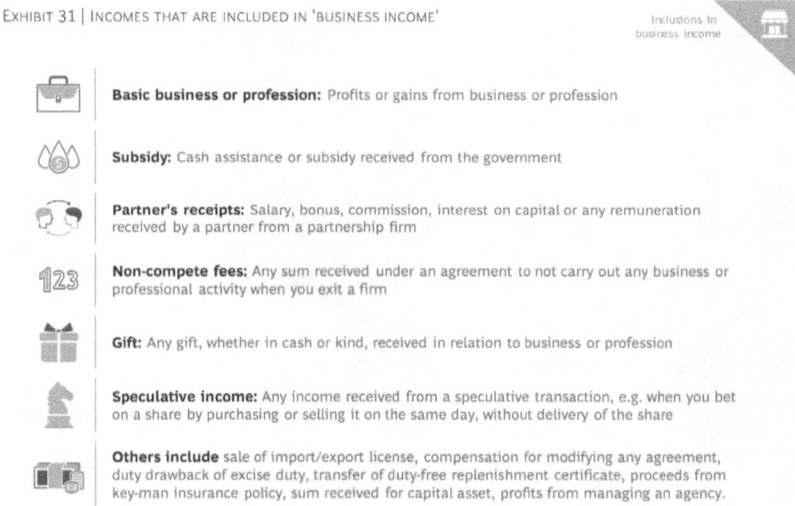

EXHIBIT 31 | INCOMES THAT ARE INCLUDED IN 'BUSINESS INCOME'

Basic business or profession: Profits or gains from business or profession

Subsidy: Cash assistance or subsidy received from the government

Partner's receipts: Salary, bonus, commission, interest on capital or any remuneration received by a partner from a partnership firm

Non-compete fees: Any sum received under an agreement to not carry out any business or professional activity when you exit a firm

Gift: Any gift, whether in cash or kind, received in relation to business or profession

Speculative income: Any income received from a speculative transaction, e.g. when you bet on a share by purchasing or selling it on the same day, without delivery of the share

Others include sale of import/export license, compensation for modifying any agreement, duty drawback of excise duty, transfer of duty-free replenishment certificate, proceeds from key-man insurance policy, sum received for capital asset, profits from managing an agency.

Did you know?

Income from an illegal business is also chargeable to tax under this head

Typically, a business can choose when they want to pay tax on their income – either when they receive/pay money, i.e. on a 'cash basis' of accounting or when the money is receivable/payable, i.e. 'mercantile (accrual) basis' of accounting.

4.4 How is business income taxed?

There are multiple modes in which a sole proprietorship business must pay taxes to the government. Like the taxes defined in earlier chapters, they can be classified into direct and indirect modes.

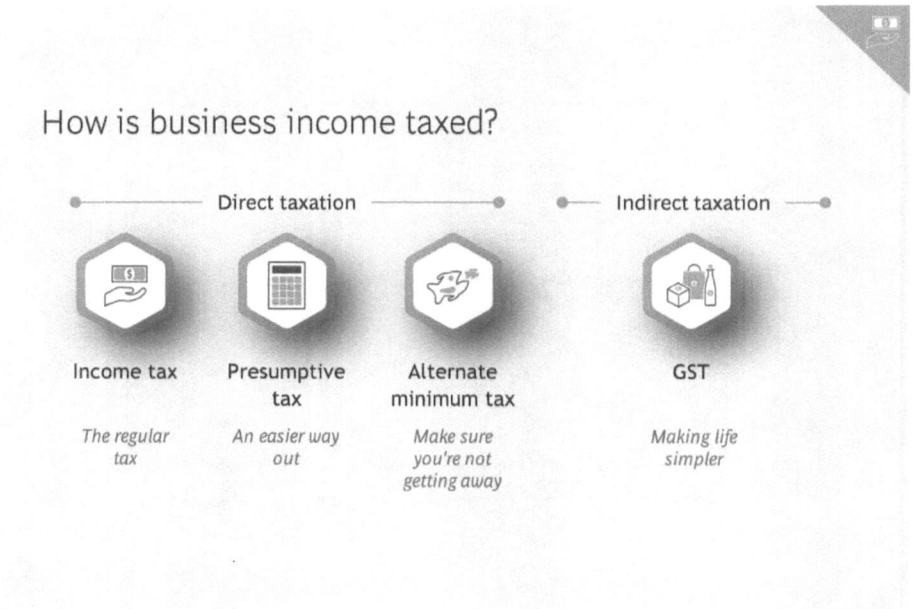

4.4.1 Direct Taxation

We learnt about the different types of persons being taxed in Chapter 1. These different persons pay tax at different rates, e.g. an individual and company, both carrying on a business, end up paying taxes at different rates. Hence, direct taxes for a business are also divided into:

1. **Income tax:** paid by persons other than registered companies, e.g. sole proprietor. These can be small and independent businesses or service providers who work for themselves in their own name. Accordingly, under direct taxation, they are taxed in their own name. Business or professional income of a sole proprietorship gets

added to the owner's individual income, after taking out related business expenses, tax deductions and other incomes if any. This is taxed based on slabs at different rates.

2. **Corporate tax:** paid by companies registered under company law in India on the net profit earned. Separate tax rates are prescribed for such companies, and these may change every year. Tax rates (excluding surcharge and cess) specified for FY 2020-21 are given below for major company types:

Particulars	FY 2020-21
Where total turnover in the year 2018-19 does not exceed Rs. 400 crores	25%
Any other domestic company	30%
Special tax rates for domestic companies[1]	
– Section 115BA: certain existing domestic manufacturing companies	25%
– Section 115BAA: certain existing domestic companies	22%
– Section 115BAB: newly set-up domestic manufacturing & electricity generation companies	15%
Foreign company	40%

1. *Note: These beneficial rates are subject to conditions prescribed in respective section*

4.4.1.1 Your regular income tax

Here, the focus is on income tax on 'Income under the head Profits and Gains from Business or Profession', which can be calculated by reducing all business or profession related expenses from total receipts. Business related expenses could be salary (if you have engaged someone), rent for the premises from where you are carrying out your profession, internet expenses, mobile expenses, official travel, lunch expenses (met officially), etc. (Exhibit 32).

EXHIBIT 32 | CALCULATION OF INCOME UNDER BUSINESS OR PROFESSION — Regular income tax

Particulars	Amount in Rs.
Gross receipts	25,00,000
(-) Business expenses	
Salary to staff	9,00,000
Rent	3,00,000
Internet and telecom	40,000
Travel expenses	2,00,000
Meals	60,000
Net Income	**10,00,000**

The above net income will be added to other taxable income. Taxes are supposed to be paid on such total income at rates applicable to the relevant income slab. You would think that calculating tax on business or profession income for an individual would be easy – however, the Income Tax Act has something else in store for you.

The Act has defined a set of incomes which may have been included in your Profit and Loss Account but are not taxable. Similarly, it has defined a set of expenses which may have been reduced to calculate annual profits from an accounting point of view – but are not allowable as expenses. There are also expenses which you would not have deducted while calculating profits but are nevertheless allowable as deduction for calculating profit or loss as per Income Tax Act.

Accordingly, such differences amongst accounting profits and taxable profits need to be taken into consideration while calculating one's tax liability.

4.4.1.2 Easier way out* - Presumptive Tax

if eligible

There is a way to avoid the complex calculations of net income as per Income Tax Act:

❖ **For Businesses**

Small businesses with turnover less than Rs. 2 crores can opt for presumptive taxation, i.e. simply declare 8% of their non-digital revenue or 6% of revenue from digital (non-cash) transactions as 'profit' and pay tax on such income. No matter the actual profit from such business.

In addition to ease of computation, such businesses are not required to maintain accounting records or get accounting records audited for tax purposes. Advance tax, if applicable, can be paid only once before 15 March of the concerned financial year, and not quarterly.

❖ **For Professionals**

Professionals (engineers, lawyers, architects, accountants, doctors, technical consultants, interior decorator, etc. who are not salaried employees), with total annual revenue up to Rs 50 lakhs, can opt for the presumptive taxation, i.e. straightaway offer 50% of total revenue as taxable income and pay taxes as per slab rates on such income. Once this scheme is opted, no expenses can be claimed as deduction.

Just like businesses, professionals opting for this scheme do not have to maintain accounting records for tax purposes.

The advantage is not just ease of computation; this scheme can also be used for tax saving:

Example: Surabhi is a practicing Chartered Accountant and has an annual income of 30 lakhs in FY 2017-18. Actual expenses incurred by her amount to 3 lakhs. Tax liability for Surabhi under both options is as follows:

Particulars	Tax liability under Presumptive tax (INR)	Tax liability under normal income tax (INR)
Income	3,000,000	3,000,000
Expenses	1,500,000	300,000
Profit	1,500,000*	2,700,000
Tax liability as per slab (excluding cess)	262,500	622,500

*50% of income is eligible for deduction

4.4.1.3 Make sure you're not getting away – Minimum Alternate Tax or Alternate Minimum Tax

There is a history to the introduction of the 'Minimum Tax' concept. Initially, this was introduced to catch companies who would take advantage of deductions and incentives applicable to them and become effectively 'zero tax' companies or end up paying only marginal tax even though they could pay normal tax. The government also needed a regular flow of tax, which was hampered by presence of such zero tax companies.

Both things were important – to maintain the sanctity of deductions or incentives given as well as payment of tax by such zero tax / marginal tax companies. Accordingly, the concept of Minimum Alternate Tax (MAT) was introduced for companies – to collect some minimum tax from them in years where normal tax liability was lower.

Minimum Alternate Tax

Applicable **only** to companies, taxes paid in a given year will be higher of:

- ❖ Normal tax payable as per applicable tax rate and surcharge, if any; or

- ❖ 15% of the book profits (plus surcharge and education cess); effective MAT rate is 15.6% - 17.472%

Unfortunately, things are never as easy as they seem. While 'book profits' may sound inconspicuous, it involves making significant adjustments to the net profit calculated from the P&L (Exhibit 33).

However, there is some relief! In case a company ends up paying higher MAT for a given year, MAT Credit to the extent of tax paid as per MAT calculation - Income tax payable under normal provisions can be carried forward for another 15 years.

Tax Type	Income / Book Profits (INR)	Tax burden (INR)
Normal tax (A)	40,00,000	12,48,000 *(30% tax + cess)*
MAT (B)	90,00,000	14,04,000 *(15% tax + cess)*
MAT Credit (B)-(A)		1,56,000

EXHIBIT 33 | MAJOR ADJUSTMENTS MADE TO NET PROFIT AS PER P&L TO ARRIVE AT BOOK PROFITS AS PER MAT

Add back items deducted from P&L

1. **Income tax** paid or payable
2. **Dividend** proposed or paid
3. Transfer made **to any reserve**
4. **Depreciation** including depreciation on account of revaluation of assets
5. Provision for **loss of subsidiary cos.**
6. Provision for **unascertained liabilities**, e.g. bad debts
7. Amount/ provision of **deferred tax**
8. Expenses relating to **exempt incomes**[1]
9. Provision for **diminution in asset value**
10. Expense relating to **royalty income** (S. 115BBF)

Deduct items added to P&L

1. **Exempt incomes** (under S. 10, 11, 12)[1]
2. Amount **withdrawn from any reserves** or provisions
3. Lower of brought forward **business loss** or **unabsorbed depreciation**
4. Amount **withdrawn from revaluation reserve** & credited to P&L
5. **Deferred tax** credited to P&L
6. **Depreciation** debited to P&L[2]
7. Income by way of **royalty** (S. 115BBF)

1. Under sections 10, 11, 12 (except S. 10AA and S. 10(38). This means that income under S. 10AA and long-term capital gain exempt under S. 10(38) are subject to MAT
2. Excluding extra depreciation due to revaluation

Alternate Minimum Tax

To avoid this, many companies began to convert themselves into partnerships. As a counteractive measure, the government had to introduce similar provisions for LLPs also – and 'Alternate Minimum Tax' (AMT) was born. Subsequently, its scope was widened to include 'every person other than a company'.

Now, all non-corporate persons who have income under the head 'Profits or Gains of Business or Profession' **and** have claimed the following deductions come within AMT's scope:

1. Certain deductions under Chapter VI-A, e.g. for profits and gains of specific industries such as hotel business, small scale industrial undertaking, housing projects, export business, infrastructure development etc.

2. Section 35AD (100% deduction on capital expenditure for specified businesses such as operation of cold chain facility, fertilizer production etc.)

3. Deductions claimed by units in Special Economic Zones (SEZs) ranging from 50% to 100%

AMT is a tax, at the rate of 18.5%, levied on 'adjusted total income' (ATI) in a financial year wherein tax on normal income is lower than AMT on ATI. ATI is calculated by adding back all the deductions mentioned above to taxable income.

So, irrespective of normal tax, AMT must be paid by taxpayers to whom AMT provisions apply. However, there is an exemption for individuals, Hindu Undivided Family (HUF), Association of Persons (AOP), Body of Individuals (BOI) and artificial juridical person whose ATI does not exceed Rs 20 lakhs. Moreover, like MAT Credit, AMT Credit (excess of AMT paid over normal income tax liability) can be carried forward up to 15 years succeeding the FY in which such AMT is paid and reduced against normal tax to the extent of the difference between normal tax and AMT.

4.4.2 Indirect Taxation

Back in Chapter 1, we saw how a plethora of taxes such as excise duty, customs duty, service tax, central sales tax, value added tax (VAT), entry tax, purchase tax, entertainment tax, tax on lottery, betting and gambling, luxury tax, tax on advertisements, etc. were charged as indirect taxes.

For small or medium sized businesses, owners or manufacturers had to take care of such different taxes and run to various departments to fulfil all tax-related documentation. Some file different taxes biannually, annually, half-yearly, etc. The more the departments, the more is the effort.

GST was introduced as a way of reducing complications and bringing in symmetry by consolidating many such indirect taxes into one tax. Now, one of the primary indirect taxes to be dealt with by businesses or professionals is GST. Just a reminder from Chapter 1 to refresh your memory! (Exhibit 3).

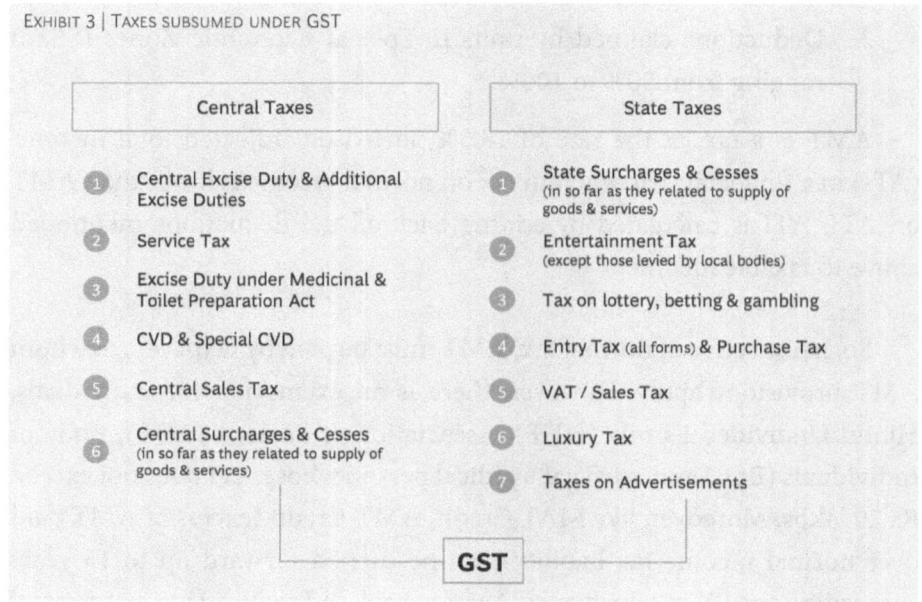

EXHIBIT 3 | TAXES SUBSUMED UNDER GST

4.4.2.1 Making life simpler – GST

Basics of GST

GST is a tax on consumption, i.e. final liability to pay GST is on end-consumers like us. We noted earlier that different states had different indirect tax regimes which were replaced by one central tax called GST. However, both Central and State Governments have their own responsibilities to perform for which they need to raise tax revenue. State governments still need their revenues. To protect states' revenue, GST is levied simultaneously by the Centre and States, depending on whether the transaction is within the same state or between two states:

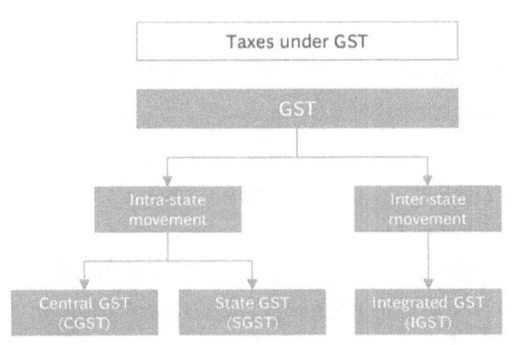

CGST | Central GST, as the name suggests, is levied by the Central Government on supplies within the same state

SGST | State CGST, similarly, is governed by the respective State Governments on supplies within the state

IGST | Integrated GST is levied on all supplies between two states, and on any supply of goods and/or services in case of import into / export from India. This tax is shared between the Centre and States

Input Tax Credit

Every registered person can take credit of the GST paid on goods or services used in the course of business, subject to other terms and conditions. This is known as 'Input Tax Credit' and is critical to avoid double taxation on products and services. It is in line with the concept of taxing on the 'value added' by a person.

Input tax credit of all three above taxes can be taken to pay out CGST, SGST and IGST as follows:

To pay IGST	• Input tax credit from IGST, CGST & SGST paid on purchases
To pay CGST	• Input tax credit from CGST & IGST paid on purchases
To pay SGST	• Input tax credit from SGST & IGST paid on purchases

Example:

Let us consider that goods worth Rs. 10,000 are sold by manufacturer A from Maharashtra to Dealer B in Maharashtra.

* Dealer B resells them to Trader C in Rajasthan for Rs. 17,500.

* Trader C finally sells to end user D in Rajasthan for Rs. 30,000.

* Suppose the applicable tax rates for the goods sold are CGST= 9%, SGST=9%, and IGST=9+9=18%

* Since A is selling this to B in Maharashtra itself, it is an intra-state sale and so, CGST at 9% and SGST at 9% will apply.

* Dealer B (Maharashtra) is selling to Trader C (Rajasthan). Hence, this is an interstate sale, with IGST at 18%.

* Trader C (Rajasthan) is selling to end user D also in Rajasthan. Once again it is an intra-state sale and hence, CGST at 9% and SGST at 9% will apply.

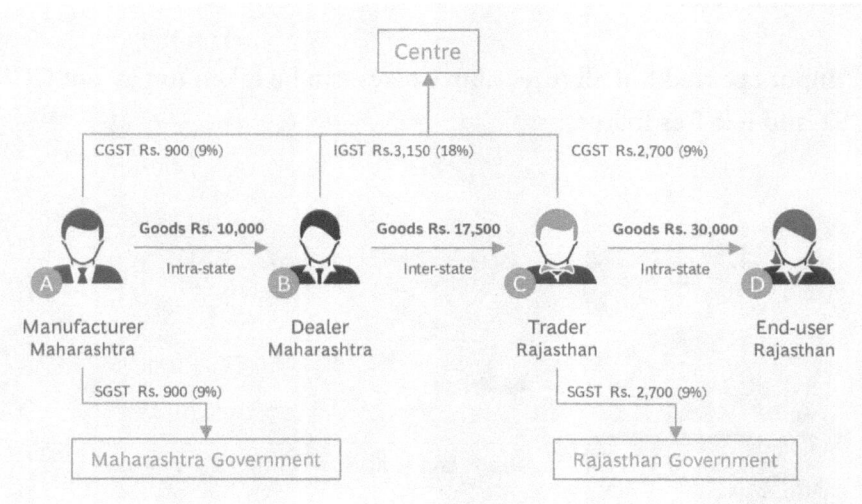

So how does this work in the back end?

Step	Transaction	Sale Price (INR)	Amount received as tax by					
			Maharashtra		Rajasthan		Centre	
1	A to B	10,000	10,000*9% (SGST)	900	-		10,000*9%	900
2	B to C	17,500	-		-		17,500*18% (IGST)	3,150
							(-) CGST credit (paid to A)	(900)
							(-) SGST credit (paid to A)	(900)
							Net	1,350
3	C to D	30,000	-		30,000*9% (SGST)	2,700	30,000*9% (CGST)	2,700
					(-) IGST credit balance (3,150 - 2,700)	(450)	(-) IGST credit	(2,700)
					Net	2,250	Net	-
	Total receipts			900		2,250		2,250
4	Adjustment		Transfer to centre	(900)	Transfer from centre	450	Net transfer	450
	Final			-		2,700		2,700

Given GST is a consumption-based tax, the state where the goods are finally consumed will receive GST, i.e. Rajasthan and the state where goods were sold, i.e. Maharashtra should not get any tax. The Central Government and Rajasthan State should have split the GST revenue equally. Accordingly, Maharashtra (exporting state) will have to transfer credit of SGST of Rs. 900 (used in payment of IGST) to the Centre. In turn, Central Government will transfer to state Rajasthan (importing state) Rs. 450 IGST reduced as credit from the state's revenue.

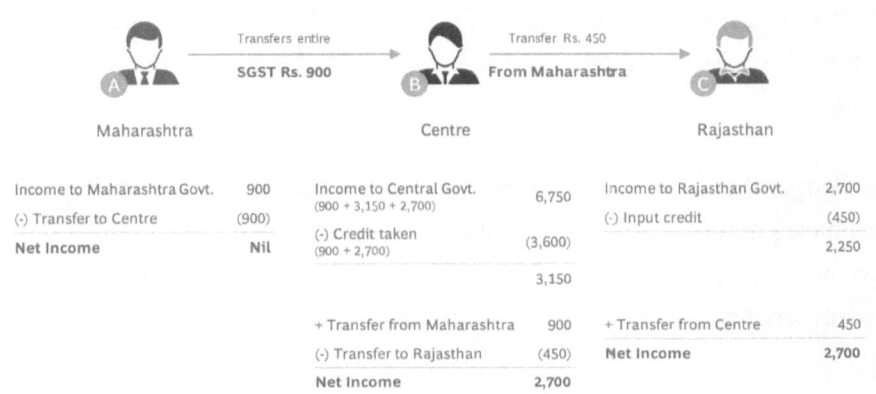

Income to Maharashtra Govt.	900	
(-) Transfer to Centre	(900)	
Net Income	Nil	

Income to Central Govt. (900 + 3,150 + 2,700)		6,750
(-) Credit taken (900 + 2,700)		(3,600)
		3,150
+ Transfer from Maharashtra		900
(-) Transfer to Rajasthan		(450)
Net Income		2,700

Income to Rajasthan Govt.	2,700
(-) Input credit	(450)
	2,250
+ Transfer from Centre	450
Net Income	2,700

Registration

Any person who supplies goods or services taxable under GST Law must get registered in their respective State or Union Territory from where such supply is carried out, if total revenue was more than Rs. 20 lakhs per year. This limit was reduced to Rs. 10 lakhs for special states – Arunachal Pradesh, Assam, Jammu and Kashmir, Mizoram, Meghalaya, Sikkim, Tripura, Manipur, Nagaland, Himachal Pradesh and Uttarakhand.

The above limits have been revised to Rs. 40 lakhs for normal category states and Rs. 20 lakhs for special category states only in case of supply of goods from 1 April 2019. However, hilly and North Eastern states were given an option. They could either choose Rs. 20 lakhs or Rs. 40 lakhs as the turnover limit for GST exemption in case of supply of goods.

Composition levy

The concept of composition levy is to provide relief to small taxable persons, i.e. suppliers of goods whose total revenue is below Rs 1.5 crore (Lower limit in case of North Eastern states and Himachal Pradesh to be notified).

It is has now been proposed that Service Providers can opt into the Composition Tax Scheme provided their annual turnover is up to Rs. 50 lakhs.

People that cannot opt for this scheme include ice cream, pan masala, or tobacco manufactures, ones that make inter-state supplies, casual taxable persons or non-residents and businesses which supply goods through an e-commerce operator (e.g. those with their products listed on Amazon).

Under this scheme, relief to taxpayers is in the form of:

1. Lesser compliance (returns, maintaining books of record, issuance of invoices)
2. Limited tax liability, as rates of tax are as low as 1% for manufactures, 5% for restaurants and 6% for service providers
3. High liquidity as taxes are at a lower rate

However, disadvantages of opting for this scheme are:

1. Limited territory of business, i.e. dealers cannot carry out transactions between two states
2. No input tax credit on goods or services purchased
3. Taxpayers cannot charge tax from their customers
4. Taxpayers cannot supply exempted goods or goods through an e-commerce portal

In every invoice raised by such a dealer, the words "composition taxable person, not eligible to collect tax on supplies" must be mentioned at the top.

Invoicing and e-invoicing

Every dealer registered under GST must provide GST Invoices, also known as bills, with a list of goods sent or services received to their clients. These invoices must adhere to the rules under GST law, i.e. include all mandatory fields and be issued within specified time limits.

In cases where dealers cannot charge GST to customers, i.e. those who have opted for the composition scheme or are supplying exempt goods, a 'bill of supply' is to be issued instead of an invoice. The only difference is that the bill of supply does not contain any tax amount.

Recently, a system of e-invoicing has been proposed for a specified class of people with turnover above Rs 100 crores, mandatorily from 1 April

2020. 'E-invoicing' or 'electronic invoicing' is a system in which invoices from one business to another are authenticated electronically by the GST Network. The biggest benefits of this system are transparency and proof.

Today, a transaction between the supplier and recipient is done directly without the government having any proof of the exchange. With e-invoicing, the moment an invoice is made, it will be uploaded to GSTN (GST Network) portal where pre-validation will be done, and a unique number called IRN (Invoice Reference Number) will be issued. Once IRN is issued, the tax invoice will be shared with the recipient also. The process is explained in detail below[6]:

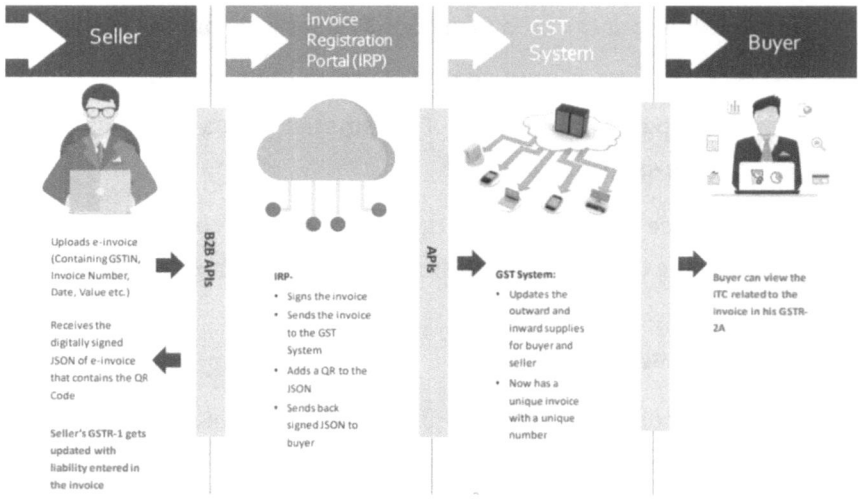

Source : https://www.gstn.org.in/

---

6   E-Invoice (IRN) System - GSTN

The GST portal has released two types of e-invoice templates. One template is only with mandatory fields and the other is with both mandatory and optional fields. This template will give a view of how an e-invoice will look like with only mandatory fields (Exhibit 34).

EXHIBIT 34 | E-INVOICE FORMAT WITH MANDATORY FIELDS ONLY (HIGHLIGHTED GREEN)

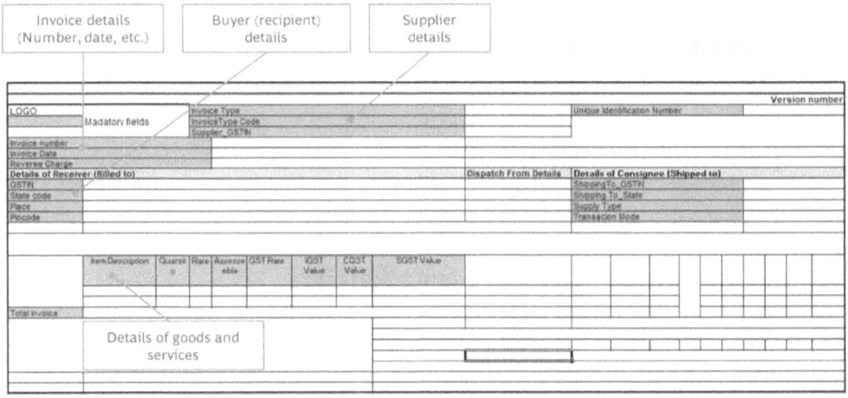

This further boosts automation in filing GST returns since filing currently involves immense manual work that is prone to errors. E-invoicing can bring ease, speed and accuracy to this process. Once the IRN is issued, it will update the records of the Supplier and, if e-waybill is required to be issued, that portal will be updated too. It will also update the records of the recipient.

From an eligible taxpayer's point of view, the ERP systems will need to be reconfigured to incorporate E-invoicing standards and have mandatory invoice parameters. At a future date, when E-invoicing applies to small taxpayers, they can choose from different accounting and billing software tied up with the GSTN, available free of cost.

That's not all! For such suppliers with total annual turnover exceeding Rs 500 crore, a QR code must be displayed on B2C invoices raised with details of:

- GSTIN of the supplier
- GSTIN of the recipient
- Invoice number given by the supplier
- Date of the generation of invoice
- Invoice value
- Number of line items
- HSN Code of the main item
- Unique Invoice Reference Number/Hash

The e-invoicing system also requires invoices printed to have a space for QR codes.

eWay Bill

No GST registered person can transport goods in a vehicle whose value exceeds Rs. 50,000 (in a single invoice) without an eWay bill generated on ewaybillgst.gov.in, or the eWay Bill Portal, barring certain exceptions.

4.5 Treading with caution

4.5.1 Expenses that can be disallowed

While computing the profit and gains from business or profession, there are certain expenditures which are disallowed, i.e. benefit of such expenditures is not allowed while computing tax liability. There are two primary reasons for disallowance of any expenditure:

1. The expenditure does not relate to the business or profession; or
2. Tax amount required to be deducted on certain expenditures is not deducted on payment

Moreover, there are certain transactions where payment for expenses is made in cash instead of cheque or bank transfer. In cases where amount of such payment exceeds Rs. 10,000, the expenditure is disallowed (with some exceptions). *Note: this applies to payments made to a single person in a single day.*

Summary of such expenses is given in Exhibit 35.

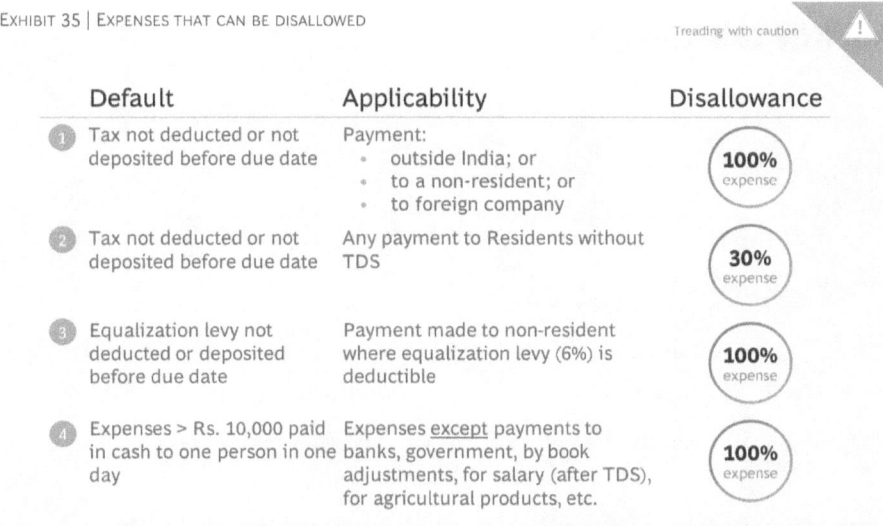

EXHIBIT 35 | EXPENSES THAT CAN BE DISALLOWED

Default	Applicability	Disallowance
① Tax not deducted or not deposited before due date	Payment: • outside India; or • to a non-resident; or • to foreign company	100% expense
② Tax not deducted or not deposited before due date	Any payment to Residents without TDS	30% expense
③ Equalization levy not deducted or deposited before due date	Payment made to non-resident where equalization levy (6%) is deductible	100% expense
④ Expenses > Rs. 10,000 paid in cash to one person in one day	Expenses except payments to banks, government, by book adjustments, for salary (after TDS), for agricultural products, etc.	100% expense

In case of TDS/ Equalization levy defaults, expenditure (except payment of salary to non-resident or person outside India) is allowable as a deduction in the year in which it is deposited with the government.

4.5.2 Accepting and repaying loans and deposits

Be careful when you take a loan or deposit from someone! If the total amount of loan or deposit taken from the same person is Rs. 20,000 or more, it cannot be in cash, i.e. the amount should be taken by cheque, bank draft, or electronically. The same rule applies for repayment of loans or deposits too. What happens if you don't follow this norm? The Joint Commissioner of Income Tax would be well within their rights to levy a penalty on you – this can go up to the amount of loan or deposit.

4.5.3 Acceptance of certain payments

Wouldn't it be nice to run a business with annual sales greater than Rs. 50 crores? (It's a big deal for us, no doubt). In case you are fortunate enough for your turnover to exceed this limit, ensure that you provide a facility for accepting payments electronically starting from the immediate next year.

4.6 Key takeaways

Exhibit 36 | Key takeaways from chapter 4

Entrepreneurship is the backbone of Indian economy; however out of individual income tax, average business income (**4.13 lakhs**) is lower than salaried income (**6.9 lakhs**)[1]; business income returns have grown at **5% CAGR** vs salaried returns at **15% CAGR** (since FY 2014-15)

Major taxes paid by a sole proprietorship business are **direct**, i.e. corporate income tax, presumptive tax for eligible businesses and MAT/AMT, and **indirect**, i.e. GST

Presumptive taxation is an option for eligible, small businesses/ professions to avoid complex tax calculations (tax on business profit: **8%** of non-digital/**6%** of digital revenue, professionals' taxable income: 50% of total revenue) and maintain fewer records

MAT/AMT (**15%** or **18.5%** of book profits / ATI plus surcharge & cess) are levied on companies or non-corporates respectively to ensure some minimum tax is paid by them, with exceptions

GST is a consumption-based tax, introduced to streamline the indirect tax regime and **consolidate multiple indirect taxes** (e.g. service tax, VAT, central excise duty[2], etc.) into one

GST is a tax **based on value added by a manufacturer or trader**, and is ultimately passed on to the consumers (who pay GST on the total amount of good/ service)

1. AY 2018-19; 2. Excise duty is levied only on certain products post-GST, i.e. petroleum products, diesel, natural gas, tobacco and alcohol

◆ CHAPTER 5 ◆

OTHER INCOMES THAT DEMAND ATTENTION

5.1 Introduction

So far, we have covered two important income types which are taxed – profits from business/ profession and salary income. However, as we (very) briefly touched upon in Chapter 1, there are other incomes which cannot escape the direct tax net! These are income from house property, capital gains and (the widely scoped) income from other sources.

The nature of these incomes is very different from what we've been looking at, e.g. salary income or profits from business/profession are typically the most important source of income that sustain your livelihood. Income from house property can be an additional source of income as you rent out your house, while capital gains and other income sources are one-off in nature. It is still important to understand the common 'other incomes' and their tax treatment, which we may come across from time to time, if not daily.

5.2 Other incomes that demand attention – an overview

Let's understand other incomes, and why they demand our attention, in a simpler way – imagine you own a house. Since you're imagining, why don't you imagine owning two houses. You stay in one house on your own and rent the other one out to a close friend.

1. **Income from house property:** The property you stay in is called 'self-occupied' property. The house you've rented out to your friend

is called 'Let-out' property. Any rental income you receive from your friend on House #2 is taxed under this head of income.

(Note: in case your imagination is going wild and you own more than two properties for your own / family's residence, any two properties are called 'self-occupied' and the others are called 'deemed let-out' properties, and 'deemed' income thereon is taxed)

2. **Income from capital gains:** Let's say you sell your House #1. Any profit from the sale (after some mathematics) is called 'capital gain', and tax is levied thereon. Capital assets that fall under this head include land (other than rural agricultural land), building, house property, vehicles, patents, trademarks, leasehold rights, machinery, and even jewelry. However, rest assured your personal goods such as clothes and furniture are not included.

Capital assets are further classified based on time duration, i.e. how many months you have been holding on to them for. This classification is important since tax rates on 'Income from capital gain' vary depending on the type of capital asset (Exhibit 37).

EXHIBIT 37 | CLASSIFICATION OF CAPITAL ASSETS AND APPLICABLE TAX RATES

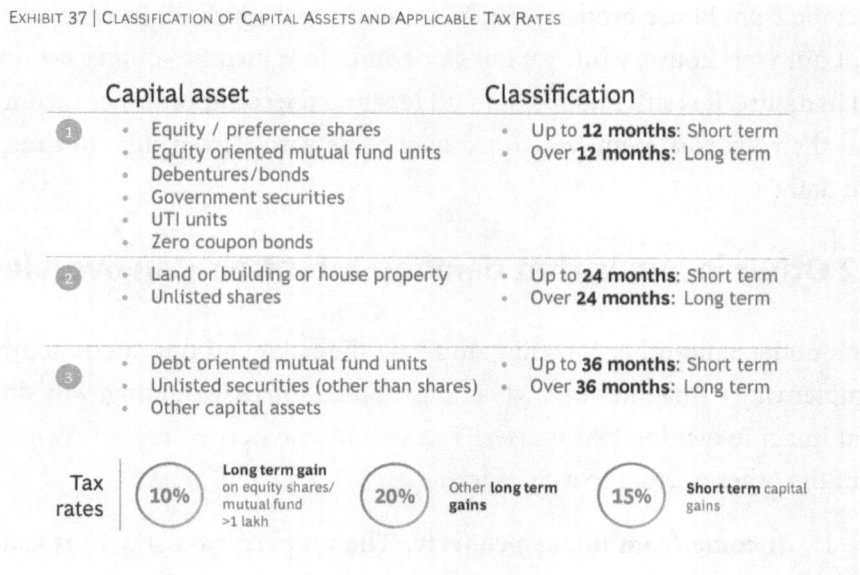

3. **Other incomes:** Your friend, grateful to you for letting them stay, gives you Rs. 55,000 as a thank you gift. Such gifts, or other incomes which don't fall under any of the income categories we discussed, fall under 'Other sources' and are also taxed. So, you'll have only a portion of that gift left in your bank account.

For ease of understanding other direct taxes, we have given examples of few common transactions below.

5.3 Direct taxes related to your house

Let's get into more detail on the above example of owning two houses and giving one on rent. You eventually sell the house given on rent later. We'll analyze the tax implications of earning rent on house property and making a profit on sale of house property.

5.3.1 Rent on house property

On House #1 (occupied by you): Since you don't receive any income from this house, there are no tax consequences to be complied with, apart from other local authority taxes like property tax, water tax etc. However, you can still claim deductions from zero income on any home loan interest for construction or purchase of the house property paid during the year, up to Rs. 2 lakhs.

Let's assume a few things on House #2:

- Rs. 40,000 rent received per month
- Rs.25,000 paid as property taxes in November
- Rs.8,000 spent on repairs
- Rs.30,000 paid in electricity bills
- Rs.2,20,000 paid as interest on money borrowed to build the house

Steps to calculate income from house property:

a. Gross Annual Value (GAV) of the property: Rent collected for a house on rent

b. Property Tax: Property tax, when paid, is allowed as a deduction from GAV of property

c. Net Annual Value (NAV) : Net Annual Value = Gross Annual Value − Property Tax

d. Reduce 30% of NAV towards standard deduction. No other expenses such as painting, and repairs can be claimed as tax relief beyond the 30% cap under this section.

e. Reduce home loan interest: Deduction is also available for interest paid during the year on housing loan availed up to Rs. 2 lakhs on self-occupied property and no limits for let-out property

f. The resulting value is your income from house property. This is taxed at the slab rate applicable to you.

Note on House #1: since its GAV is zero, claiming the deduction on home loan interest will result in a loss from house property. This loss can be adjusted against income from other heads during the year.

Particulars	INR
Gross Annual Value	480,000
Less: Property taxes	(25,000)
Net Annual Value	455,000
Less: Standard deduction at 30%	(136,500)
Less: Interest on money borrowed	(220,000)
Income from house property	**98,500**

5.3.2 Sale of house property

Since you've sold House #1 (and we're assuming you are not in the business of buying and selling houses otherwise you're in the wrong head of income), any profit/loss on sale is charged to tax as capital gains.

Steps to calculate income under capital gains:

Short term capital gain (STCG)	Step 1: Start with the total amount received on sale ('Full value consideration')
	Step 2: Deduct:
	a. Expenditure(s) incurred for such transfer
	b. Value at which you acquired the house (without adjusting for any inflation)
	c. Cost of improvement, if any
Long term capital gain (LTCG)	Step 1: Start with the full value of consideration
	Step 2: Deduct:
	- Expenditure incurred for such transfer
	- Indexed cost of acquisition: acquired value adjusted for inflation using the cost inflation index (CII)
	- Cost of improvement adjusted for inflation using CII
	Step 3: From this resulting number, deduct exemptions provided under:
	- Section 54: Money from sale of one house property invested in another house property
	- Section 54EC: Money from sale of any other capital asset invested in one house property
	- Section 54F: Money from sale of house property invested in specified bonds

Let's make the following assumptions:

- House purchased in 2007 for Rs. 80 lakhs (this qualifies as long term!)
- You're moving to another city and you sell it on 16.05.2020 for Rs.1.30 crores
- You advertised this sale in the newspaper for Rs.10,000

Note: CII 2007-08 is 129, CII 2020-21 is 301

Particulars	INR
Sale consideration	13,000,000
Less: Direct expenses	(10,000)
Net sale consideration	12,990,000
Less: Indexed cost of acquisition (80 lakhs x 301 / 129)	(18,666,667)
Less: Indexed cost of improvement	-
Long term capital gain/loss	**(5,676,667)**

This long-term capital loss can only be set-off against long term capital gains. Likewise, if it were short term capital loss, it could only be set off against short term capital gains.

5.4 Direct taxes related to your investments

Any average Indian would typically invest excess cash in at least one of the following income-generating avenues – fixed deposit, savings bank account, shares, mutual funds, debentures or bonds. There are many other modes of investing your hard-earned money, but let's start with the tax treatment on these.

5.4.1 Income from investments (shares, debentures, deposits)

Money is not free. Money has a time value. This means that money is generally not given without any expectation of anything in return (we'll come to the exceptions later). Therefore, when money is given to third parties, more often than not one expects a certain amount of return on the same. That expectation will vary depending on the risk of the investment, i.e. high-risk investments generally give higher return (e.g. equity shares) than low risk investments (e.g. bank fixed deposit).

This return on investment is also an income which needs to be disclosed to tax authorities and tax on the same needs to be paid. However, tax treatment of different investments and their incomes varies (Exhibit 38).

EXHIBIT 38 | RETURNS ON TYPICAL INVESTMENTS AND THEIR TAX TREATMENT

Investment	Return	Head of income	Taxability	Deductions
• Equity/ preference shares • Mutual funds	Dividend	Income from other sources	Fully added to income	N.A. (Refer Note)
• Fixed deposit	Interest			Up to Rs. 1.5 lakhs (Section 80C)[1]
• Debentures/ Bonds	Interest			Certain bonds under Section 80C[2]
• Savings bank account	Interest			Rs.10,000/ Rs.50,000 (Section 80TTA/80TTB)[3]

Note: Before Budget 2020, tax was deducted at distribution (DDT) from dividends on shares and mutual funds. Dividend on shares was not taxable up to Rs. 10 lakhs p.a. and was exempt on mutual funds. **DDT has been abolished in Budget 2020** and now, recipients of dividend must pay tax as per their slab rates.

1. Check eligibility of the same before investing
2. Some bonds, e.g. NABARD Bonds, Infrastructure Bonds, etc. are eligible for deduction under Section 80C
3. Rs. 50,000 is available for senior citizens aged 60 years and above

5.4.2 Sale of investments – equity shares

If you recollect, we spoke about investments in equity shares falling under 'capital assets'. Accordingly, any profit or loss on sale of investments will also attract tax under the head capital gains. The same will be categorized as long term or short term depending on the duration of investment (Refer Exhibit 37 above).

However, that is not always the case. There has been certain (read: a lot) of debate around whether profit on sale of equity shares can be treated as capital gains or business income. In case of significant trading activity (e.g. if you trade daily or engage in daily Futures and Options), usually your income is classified as income from business.

When you treat the sale of shares as **business income**, expenses incurred in earning such business income are reduced. The profit is added to your total income and is charged at slab rates. If you treat your income as **capital gains**, expenses incurred on transfer are deductible (like we did for the sale of house property above). Also, as mentioned above, long term gains from equity above Rs 1 lakh annually are taxable at 10%, while short term gains are taxed at 15%. However, indexation benefit will not be available in case of LTCG on sale of equity shares/equity oriented mutual funds.

You have the option of making a choice of holding the shares as either capital assets or stock-in-trade. Carefully choose because you can't change it later!

Let's look at an example of sale of shares as a capital asset:

- Priyanka purchased shares for Rs.10,00,000 on 1st August 2018 and sold them for Rs.13,00,000 on 31st December 2019
- She paid brokerage at 0.01% and STT at 0.125% of transaction value

Particulars	INR
Sale consideration	1,300,000
Less: Direct expenses (Brokerage)	(130)
Net sale consideration	1,299,870
Less: Cost of acquisition	(1,000,000)
Long term capital gain/loss	299,870
Exempt	(1,00,000)
Taxable long-term capital gain	199,870
Tax on LTCG @ 10%	**19,987**

Note: STT paid is not deductible against capital gains but is deductible from business income.

Earlier, before Budget 2018, tax on **LTCG arising on equity shares** used to be Nil. However, the exemption was withdrawn, by grandfathering (meaning: protecting) all investments made on or before 31 January 2018. It means for sale of any investments on or after 1 April 2018, cost of acquisition shall be higher of: i) the market value as on 31 January 2018 (however, it cannot exceed sale consideration) or ii) actual cost of acquisition.

5.4.3 Sale of investments – Sovereign Gold Bonds (SGBs)

The Government introduced the Sovereign Gold Bond (SGB) Scheme in November 2015 to give investors a chance to own gold without physically owning it, i.e. in certificate form. Think of SGBs like any other debt fund – where you are paid fixed interest (2.5% in the 2020 Bonds) and are guaranteed repayment of the amount (at the market price of gold!) at the end of 8 years.

Few features of SGBs:

- **Eligibility:** Any Indian resident can purchase them – including individuals, HUFs, trusts, universities and charitable institutions
- **Tenure:** Maturity period 8 years, i.e. the government will redeem it at the end of 8 years at the gold market price; lock in period: 5 years, i.e. after 5 years you can choose to exit by selling the SGB to another person
- **Interest rate:** Current rate is 2.5% annual (you end up earning more than actual returns on market price of gold). This interest is **fully taxable** (like interest on other bonds/debentures).

Remember – there is no TDS on this interest. Hence, you need to pay advance taxes on this income and show it in your returns if applicable as per limits.

Let's look at what happens when you sell SGBs after 5 years vs redeem them after 8 years:

Particulars	Scenario 1	Scenario 2
	Sell after 5 years*	*Redeem after 8 years*
Nature of gain (if>3 years)	- Long term capital gain	- Long term capital gain
Tax treatment	- LTCG (if > 3years): with indexation benefit available - STCG: (if < 3years): normal treatment	- No LTCG tax; capital gains exempted

*   *in the open (secondary) market*

SGBs are low-risk investment vehicles for those interested in buying gold but not in going through the hassle of keeping the physical gold safe. Find out if they meet your financial goals – these are issued in notified tranches.

5.5 Incomes you need not pay tax on

In Chapter 3 (Salaried individuals), we read about certain exemptions on allowances that form part of salary income. In addition to those, there are other incomes for which your income tax liability is Nil subject to certain conditions. We have listed below common examples of such exempt incomes:

1. **Agricultural income:** To boost the agricultural sector, any income generated through agriculture is exempt from tax. However, note that such agriculture income is still included in total income for the limited purpose of determining the tax slab/rate.

2. **Receipts from HUF:** Receiving or inheriting money as a member of an HUF

3. **Share from a partnership firm:** any share a partner may have in the total income of the firm

4. **Scholarships:** granted to deserving students to meet the cost of education

5. **Life insurance policy:** Amount received under a life insurance policy subject to certain conditions

6. **Incomes of MP, MLA:** daily allowances of MPs and MLAs, any allowance of MPs or any constituency allowance received by an MLA

5.6 Are your gifts also taxed?

Gifts are the exception to our above statement of giving money, or anything else in kind, without expecting anything in return. We don't have a 'gift tax' in India (we did, but it was abolished in 1998 when all gifts were made tax free till 2004). However, any gifts received exceeding Rs. 50,000 are taxed in hands of the person receiving the gift under the head 'Income from Other Sources'.

A gift could be anything – money, paintings/drawings, jewellery, even a house or any other immoveable property. If you receive any such gifts for no/less than adequate consideration, keep in mind that the entire amount is taxable if it exceeds Rs. 50,000. However, there are certain gifts which are exempted from tax (Exhibit 39).

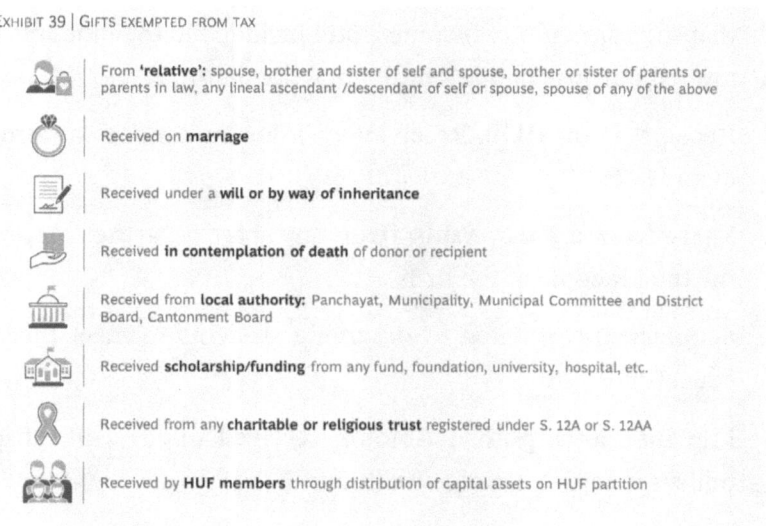

EXHIBIT 39 | GIFTS EXEMPTED FROM TAX

From **'relative'**: spouse, brother and sister of self and spouse, brother or sister of parents or parents in law, any lineal ascendant /descendant of self or spouse, spouse of any of the above

Received on **marriage**

Received under a **will or by way of inheritance**

Received **in contemplation of death** of donor or recipient

Received from **local authority**: Panchayat, Municipality, Municipal Committee and District Board, Cantonment Board

Received **scholarship/funding** from any fund, foundation, university, hospital, etc.

Received from any **charitable or religious trust** registered under S. 12A or S. 12AA

Received by **HUF members** through distribution of capital assets on HUF partition

Caution! Due to extensive tax planning using gifts, they generally fall under the scrutiny of the department, especially if the amount is large. Hence, it is good to maintain documentation to establish genuineness of the gift(s) and sufficient source of funds with the donor to justify it.

If you happen to win the lottery, or Kaun Banega Crorepati (or any other online/TV game shows etc.), it will also be taxable under the head 'Income from other Sources'. This income will be taxable at the flat rate of **30%** plus any cess.

5.7 Gaining from your losses

We've spoken so much about how your money is deducted, it's also important to cover how you stand to gain even from losses by 'setting them off'.

Set-off of losses means adjusting the losses against the profits or income of that particular year. Losses that are not set off against income in the same year can be carried forward to the subsequent years for set off against income of those years. Set-off can be within the same head of income (e.g. loss from textile business with profit from medical business) or with another head of income (e.g. house property loss with salary income, but in the same year).

This, however, comes with restrictions on setting off certain types of losses and carrying them forward to set-off against subsequent years' gains (Exhibit 40).

EXHIBIT 40 | SET-OFF AND CARRY FORWARD OF LOSSES

Type of loss	In year of loss	Subsequent years	Carry forward
House Property	• Any income, including salary[1]	• Only House Property income	8 years
Business/ Profession (non-speculative)	• Any income, excluding salary[1]	• Only profits from business/ profession	8 years
Business income (Speculative)	• Speculative income	• Speculative income	4 years
Long Term Capital loss	• Long term capital gain only	• Long term capital gain only	8 years
Short Term Capital loss	• Short term capital gain only	• Short term capital gain only	8 years
Other sources • Gambling, betting • Owning racehorses • Other incomes	• **No set-off** • Such income • Any income excluding salary[1]	• **No set-off** • Such income • Any income excluding salary[1]	4 years

1. No set-off against winning incomes (lottery, betting, gambling, etc.)

Caution! Except house property, other losses cannot be carried forward if the return is not filed within the original due date.

5.8 Be careful of other taxes too

In this chapter, we have broadly covered the direct tax implications of incomes from other typical transactions not covered previously. However, you must also be aware of the potential indirect tax impact on below common transactions.

5.8.1 Sale of house property

GST on sale

Only land

Under the GST regime, sale of land is one of the items specified in **negative list**, i.e. not included in the definition of 'supply'. Thus, GST is not applicable on sale of immovable property being land.

Building/Land and building

However, in case an **under-construction building or flat** is purchased from a **builder**, where any amount is paid to such builder before issuance of completion certificate from a competent authority, then this is considered a 'service' and will be liable to GST. Let's understand with an example:

- ❖ Akshay bought an apartment from Thakur Constructions for Rs.30 lakhs
- ❖ He paid Rs. 5 lakhs as advance at the start of construction (Of course, prior to issuance of completion certificate)
- ❖ He paid the balance amount at the time of possession of the property
- ❖ Will GST be levied on the entire Rs. 30 lakhs or Rs. 5 lakhs or nil?

Solution | Akshay paid Rs.5 lakhs before issuance of completion certificate. Hence, the **entire Rs.30 lakhs** will be liable to GST.

However, if you (assuming you're not a builder and this is not your business) plan on further selling your existing house property / flat to another buyer, it counts as your personal asset. And transfer of any personal asset is outside the ambit of GST. Hence, you will not be liable to pay GST on sale of the under constructed flat.

TDS on sale

Sale of an immovable property, other than an agricultural land, greater than or equal to Rs.50 lakhs attracts TDS. And if you are the purchaser, then you must **deduct TDS @ 1% on the sale price** at the time of payment. Not only that, you also need to remit this to the government by 7th of the next month. *(Note: you'll need to register on the incometaxindia.gov.in to obtain a Tax Deduction and Collection Account Number (TAN)).*

This TDS amount deducted by you can be adjusted with the tax payable by the supplier on filing income tax returns.

5.8.2 Rent on property

Renting of any immovable property (land, building, etc.) qualifies as a 'service', which is liable to GST at specified rates. In case any goods or services are used in providing this service, GST on those can be claimed as 'input tax credit' to the extent paid.

Once you have a tenant and the rent agreement in place, you'll need to register on the GST portal for a Goods and Services Taxpayer Identification Number (GST-IN) and comply with monthly and/or quarterly GST-returns.

5.8.3 Shares buy back

When it comes to stock investing, there are two ways in which companies offer rewards to their investors – dividends and buy-backs.

Both are given out from the distributable profits of a company; however, both differ in their meaning, purpose and tax treatment.

As we covered above, dividend is a return per share paid to the shareholders. They serve as a steady source of income, particularly for smaller shareholders. On the other hand, share buy-back is an offer from the company to buy its shares from shareholders. This is optional and is offered at a reasonable premium to the existing market price for making it more lucrative for shareholders.

Tax on buy-back (BBT) is levied by the company at the time of distribution at 20% plus applicable surcharge and cess. Accordingly, no taxes are to be paid by the shareholders on any gains on buy-back.

Before Finance Act 2020, tax was also deducted at distribution (DDT) from dividends on shares. Dividend on shares was not taxable up to Rs. 10 lakhs p.a. DDT has been abolished by Finance Act 2020 and now, recipients of dividend must pay tax as per their slab rates. However, no change was proposed in BBT rates.

This should benefit foreign investors, multinational companies (MNCs), holding companies and other investors in the lower income tax bracket. Foreign companies would have to pay anywhere around 5% -15% tax on dividends, depending on the tax treaty that India has with the country from where the investment is routed. On the other hand, it will end up hurting domestic promoters and individuals falling in the 30 per cent-plus tax bracket.

Hence, it is likely that cash-rich companies may opt for buybacks over dividends, as a promoter-friendly measure, since any gain on buy-back is exempt in the hands of the shareholders. Given below is an example to demonstrate taxability of dividends under the old regime, new regime and buy-back.

Particulars	Dividend income		Buy-back gain
	Old regime	New regime	No change
Excess cash to be distributed	1,000,000	1,000,000	1,000,000
Effective DDT/BBT rate (including surcharge and cess)	20.56%	-	23.30%
Less: DDT/BBT	(205,600)	-	(232,960)
Amount distributed	794,400	1,000,000	767,040
Tax paid by shareholders	-*	(300,000)**	-
Net cash received by shareholders	**794,400**	**700,000**	**767,040**

* It is assumed that this is being paid to a single shareholder receiving dividend up to Rs. 10 lakhs under the old regime (i.e. exempt)

** Highest tax bracket of 30% is considered for the individual; impact may vary across different tax brackets

5.9 Key takeaways

EXHIBIT 41 | KEY TAKEAWAYS FROM CHAPTER 5

 Other than salary and business income, **incomes from house property, capital gains and other income** are major groups under direct taxation

 Common transactions that attract income tax are related to capital investments, e.g. rental income from or sale of house property, income from or sale of investments in an FD, savings bank account, shares, SGBs etc.

 However, also be mindful of other taxes that come into play on these transactions, e.g. GST on sale or rent of house property, TDS on sale of immoveable property, etc.

 Earlier dividend was distributed after deducting DDT at 15% (effective rate ~20.56%) & made exempt for recipients; now, **recipients of dividend must pay tax on this as per their own slab rates** (putting higher tax bracket promoters at a disadvantage)

 Even **gifts received in cash or kind exceeding INR 50K** from others come under the tax net, albeit with exceptions

 Subject to rules, you can reduce your tax incidence by **adjusting certain losses under one head of income with incomes under the same or another head** for limited time (0-8 years)

• CHAPTER 6 •

TAX COMPLIANCES

6.1 Introduction

You have learnt a lot about tax so far and have come a long way! In theory, you know why taxes are levied, what the kinds of taxes are and how they are administered across varied types of income. But there is still one critical part we haven't covered – the practical. There are multiple 'compliances' or regular tax-chores that each one of us has to complete within given deadlines, failing which consequences follow. To avoid falling into this trap, it's better to be safe than sorry and know what is expected of us well in advance. Let's cover major direct and indirect tax compliances in this chapter.

6.2 Direct tax compliances

6.2.1 Getting your PAN card

6.2.1.1 What is a PAN card?

Think of a tax identity card for the income tax department to find you – that's your PAN card. The Permanent Account Number. Much like the Aadhaar card you stood in line to make and link to. All tax-information for a person/company is recorded against a single PAN number.

6.2.1.2 Is it mandatory for everyone?

PAN Card is issued to individuals, companies, non-resident Indians or anyone who pays taxes in India. But is it mandatory? The answer is "No".

The Income tax Act mandates requirement of a PAN card only in the following cases:

i) Where total income exceeds **applicable basic exemption** limit during the year; or

ii) Where total **sales are Rs.50,00,000 or more** in any previous year; or

iii) For a person **required to furnish an Income Tax Return (ITR)** as specified by Income tax department; or

iv) For a resident, other than individual, which enters into a **financial transaction of Rs.2,50,000** or more in a year; or

v) For the Managing Director, Director, Partner, Trustee, Author, Founder, Karta, Chief Executive Officer, Principal Officer or Office Bearer of the person referred to in above clause

6.2.1.3 How do you apply for a PAN card?

Application for a PAN is simple three-step process, moved online through the NSDL portal. Let's understand the steps of the process:

Step-1: Go to https://www.onlineservices.nsdl.com/paam/endUserRegisterContact.html

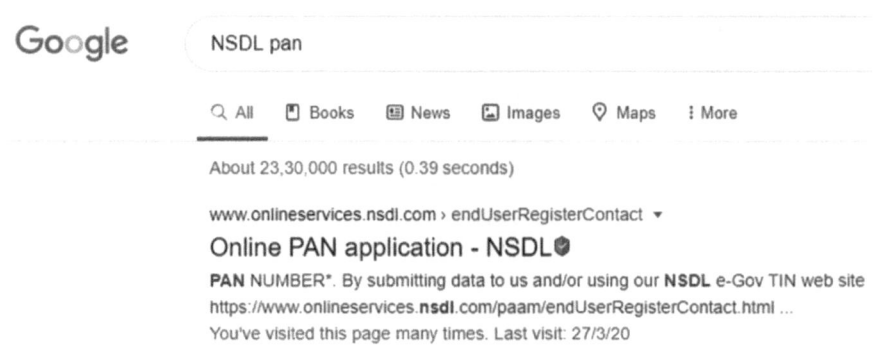

Step-2: Create a User ID and Password by filling the details. After logging in, enter personal details like name, personal and office address, etc.

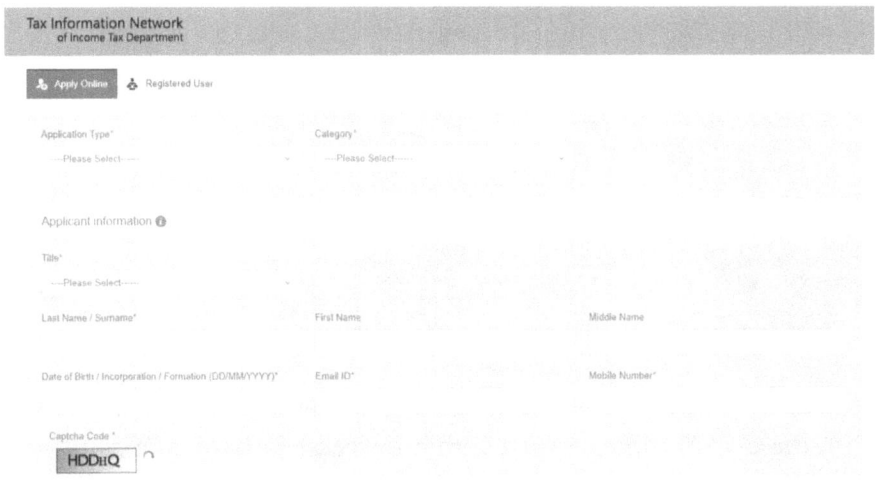

Step-3: The filled application form will be received on your registered email ID as an attachment.'

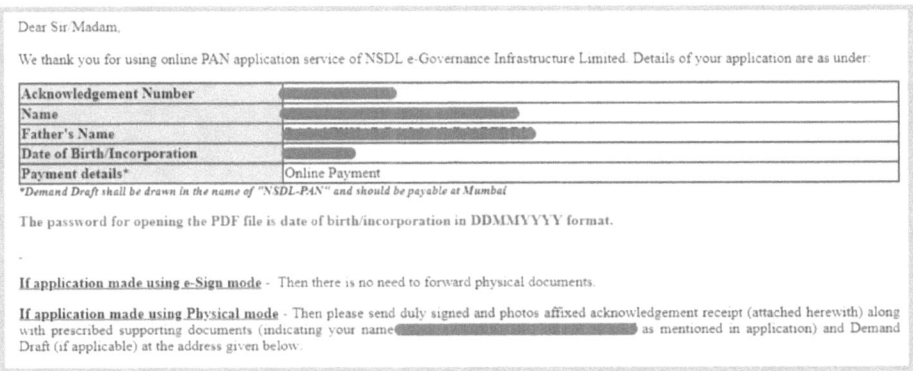

> **INCOME TAX PAN SERVICES UNIT**
> (Managed by NSDL e-Governance Infrastructure Limited)
> 4th Floor, Mantri Sterling, Plot No. 341,
> Survey No. 997/8, Model Colony,
> Near Deep Bungalow Chowk,
> Pune - 411 016
> PAN/TDS Call Centre: 020 - 27218080 | Fax: 020 - 27218081
> e-mail: tininfo@nsdl.co.in
>
> To know the details of supporting documents, please click here (Indian citizens, Foreign citizens).
>
> Your application made using physical mode will be processed after receipt of supporting documents. On receipt of your documents, an acknowledgement will be sent to you by e-mail.
>
> This is an auto generated e-mail please do not reply to this e-mail.
>
> **NSDL**
> Technology, Trust & Reach
> NSDL e-Governance Infrastructure Limited (CIN U72900MH1995PLC095642)
> 1st Floor, Times Tower, Kamala Mills Compound, Senapati Bapat Marg, Lower Parel, Mumbai - 400 013
> For status of your application, please click here or SMS NSDLPAN<space>15 digit acknowledgment no. to 57575
>
> **Caution:-** Income Tax Department does not send e-mails regarding refunds and does not seek any taxpayer information like user name, password, details of ATM, bank accounts, credit cards, etc. Taxpayers are advised not to part with such information on the basis of emails.

Thanks to the quick process of e-KYC (validation through Aadhar OTP), the e-PAN card is issued within a week and hard copy is typically received in 10-20 days.

The Income Tax Portal also has a new (and easier) procedure for applying for a PAN card (Exhibit 42).

EXHIBIT 42 | NEW PAN CARD APPLICATION PROCEDURE ON THE INCOME TAX PORTAL

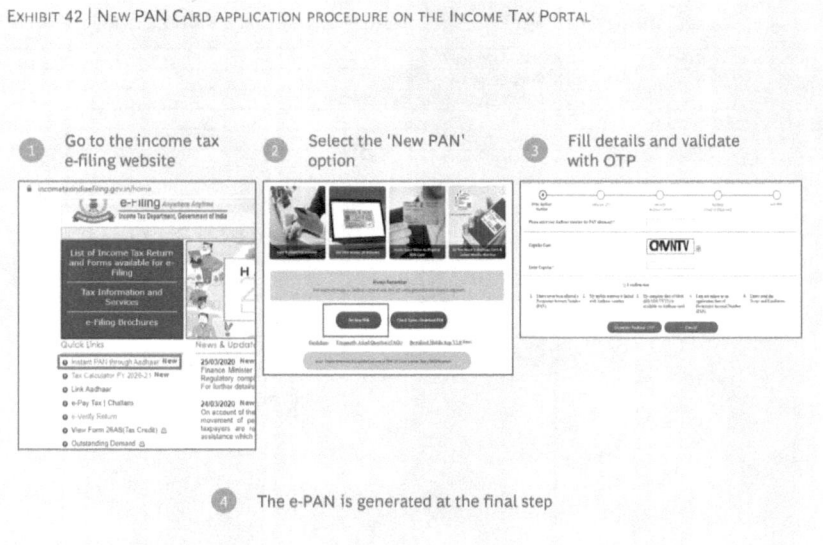

6.2.2 Acting responsibly

There are a plethora of rules and regulations to ensure that we don't game the system and remain honest in our undertakings. These are important to have because in the absence of rules there is bound to be chaos. We must follow said rules and act responsibly to avoid dire consequences such as receiving notices, attending hearings, fighting with tax authorities or paying penalties. Few important and recurring tasks that we must fulfill are given below.

6.2.2.1 Maintaining proper records

If you haven't had the chance to go through a typical accounting textbook, books of accounts are defined as the 'language of a business' in some of them. Imagine yourself keeping a daily record of your cash receipts and expenses, of all your daily transactions, of invoices raised or paid by you. Books of accounts are similar, just more organized and well structured.

On one hand, there are 'normal provisions' under the Act which lay down guidelines for maintaining such records of a business. On the other hand, previously mentioned presumptive taxation rules make life simpler in terms of maintaining these records. But why is it required? It's for the income tax officer to verify that you have, in fact, calculated your tax payable correctly.

Normal provisions

Normal provisions are rules applicable to all, unless someone has specifically opted for presumptive tax provisions. Under these, every business is required to maintain prescribed books of accounts if it fulfills any of the below conditions:

a. Annual income from business or profession >Rs. 1,20,000; or
b. Total sales >Rs. 10,00,000 in **any** of the past 3 years

If your business is newly set-up, firstly congratulations and good luck! You will have to maintain the required books of accounts in case you expect an income more than Rs. 1,20,000 during the year or sales more than Rs. 10,00,000 during the year.

The rules are different for certain specified professions, i.e. Engineering, Legal, Architectural profession, Accountant, Medical, Technical consultant and Interior decoration. For such professionals, accounting records need to be maintained if total receipts exceed Rs. 1,50,000 in **any** of the 3 previous years. For others, the limit is Rs. 2,50,000 for annual income or Rs. 25,00,000 for total receipts in **any** of the 3 previous years.

Presumptive tax provisions

As we covered briefly above, this scheme is intended to provide relief to the smaller taxpayers. Accordingly, eligible persons opting for this scheme have the benefit of not maintaining any books of accounts.

However, those who claim their income from business or profession is lower than the presumed income must maintain books of accounts and have them audited too.

Note: Each year's books must be kept for a period of 6 years from the end of that year.

What happens if you don't maintain proper records?

As with most other offences, you may be charged a penalty:

- Rs 25,000 (in a normal scenario); or
- 2% of transaction value (in case of international transactions)

Getting your books of accounts audited

The law also mandates audit of books of accounts in the following cases:

1. If business turnover exceeds Rs. 1 crore
   a. This limit is increased to Rs. 5 crores for those restricting their cash transactions, i.e. cash receipts are limited to 5% of the gross receipts or turnover **and** cash payments are limited to 5% of the aggregate payments
2. If professional receipts exceed Rs. 50 lakhs;
3. If presumptive taxation is opted for but income declared is lower than presumptive income calculated

The above is termed as a tax audit and must be conducted by a Chartered Accountant by 30 September of the relevant assessment year. The deadline is 30 November of the relevant assessment year in cases with international or specified domestic transactions (related party transactions). However, do keep a note of any announcements made in connection with due dates.

6.2.2.2 Filing income tax returns

What is an Income Tax Return (ITR)?

The term ITR was mentioned quite a few times earlier. An ITR is a declaration of the business' income, expenditure, assets and liabilities. Further, taxes payable on business profits are also self-computed and declared on the same ITR.

Who must file an ITR?

For a sole proprietor or professional earning income from business or profession, both this income and any other personal incomes like salary, house property and interest income are to be stated on the same ITR.

ITRs must be filed when total income from all sources exceeds basic exemption limit, currently Rs. 2,50,000. *(Note: you must compute total income without factoring in any deductions)*. You can voluntarily file an ITR even if your income level is below this threshold. Make sure you disclose even exempt income on your ITR.

When must an ITR be filed?

There are two primary due dates for filing ITRs:

a. For individuals for whom tax audit is **not** mandatory: 31 July after financial year end

b. For individuals for whom tax audit is mandatory: 30 September after financial year end

This due date can be occasionally extended by the CBDT – so stay tuned to the news around these dates for updates!

Belated ITR

In case you miss filing the ITR by this due date, there is the option of filing a belated ITR. This can be filed either by:

a. End of the relevant assessment year (e.g. 31 March 2021 for FY 2019-20);

b. Before completion of assessment

whichever is earlier (Exhibit 43).

What happens if you don't file your ITR?

In case you completely miss filing your ITR, you may suffer the following consequences:

1. Any loss incurred during the year cannot be carried forward if the ITR is filed after the due date

2. Interest at 1% per month or part of a month till you pay the taxes (you can't file the ITR till taxes are paid)
3. Delay in refunds, if they are due
4. Max. Rs. 10,000 late filing fees

EXHIBIT 43 | UNDERSTANDING BELATED ITR

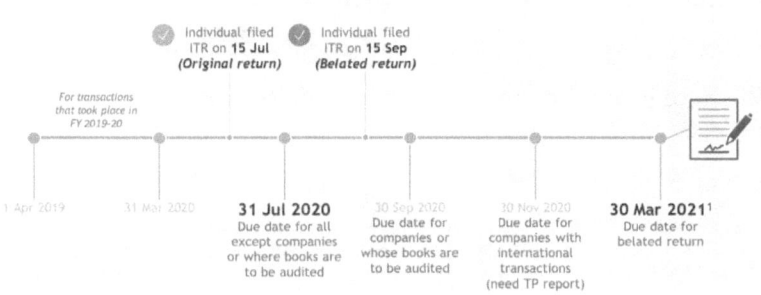

1. Where assessment is not completed; if it is, then due date for filing belated return is completion of assessment

Revised ITR

Sometimes mistakes can be made filing income tax returns: wrong bank details, incorrect personal information, wrong income tax return form, difference in income tax return income and Form 26AS, error in residential status, incorrect deduction claim, unintentional omission foreign income or foreign assets, etc.

In such cases, a revised ITR can be filed by either:

a. End of the relevant assessment year (e.g. 31 March 2021 for FY 2019-20); or
b. Before completion of assessment

whichever is earlier.

How to file an ITR?

Income tax returns have been simplified and must be e-filed by all taxpayers. You can use either of the two options:

1. Government's official Income Tax website https://www.incometaxindia.gov.in/Pages/tax-services/file-income-tax-return.aspx
2. Third party software/websites such as Taxpro, Cleartax, etc.

The income tax department notifies ITR forms for every assessment year. We have listed the broad steps to file ITRs in Exhibit 44.

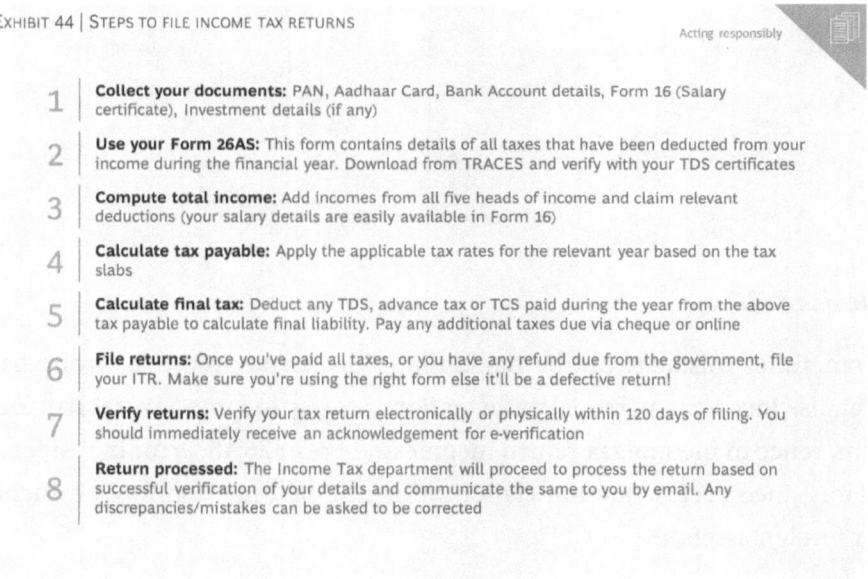

EXHIBIT 44 | STEPS TO FILE INCOME TAX RETURNS

1. **Collect your documents:** PAN, Aadhaar Card, Bank Account details, Form 16 (Salary certificate), Investment details (if any)
2. **Use your Form 26AS:** This form contains details of all taxes that have been deducted from your income during the financial year. Download from TRACES and verify with your TDS certificates
3. **Compute total income:** Add incomes from all five heads of income and claim relevant deductions (your salary details are easily available in Form 16)
4. **Calculate tax payable:** Apply the applicable tax rates for the relevant year based on the tax slabs
5. **Calculate final tax:** Deduct any TDS, advance tax or TCS paid during the year from the above tax payable to calculate final liability. Pay any additional taxes due via cheque or online
6. **File returns:** Once you've paid all taxes, or you have any refund due from the government, file your ITR. Make sure you're using the right form else it'll be a defective return!
7. **Verify returns:** Verify your tax return electronically or physically within 120 days of filing. You should immediately receive an acknowledgement for e-verification
8. **Return processed:** The Income Tax department will proceed to process the return based on successful verification of your details and communicate the same to you by email. Any discrepancies/mistakes can be asked to be corrected

We have also added screenshots of the process through the official IT website below to help simplify it.

Step-1

Go to - https://www.incometaxindiaefiling.gov.in/ and select -IT Return Preparation Software under 'Downloads'. *Note: Select the right applicable file from the below list!*

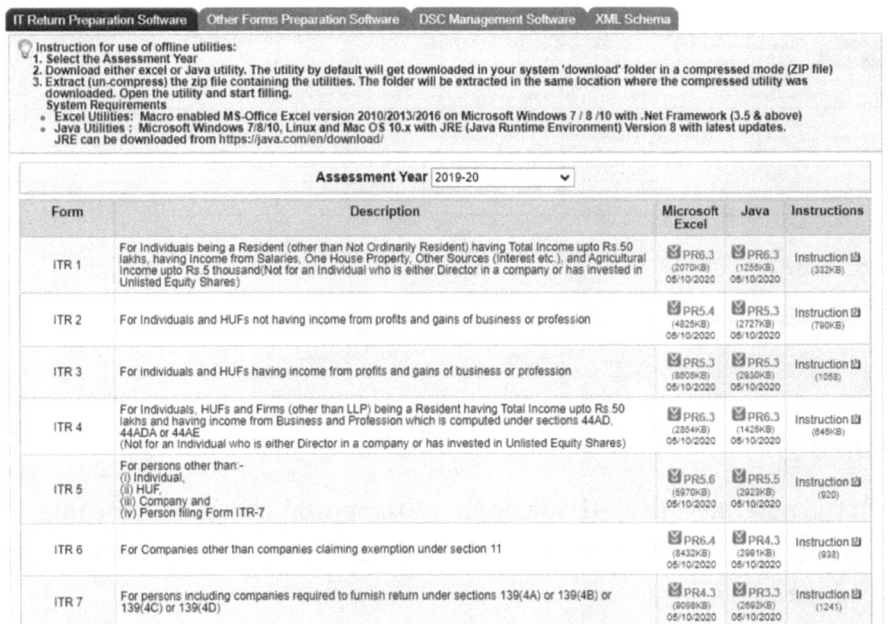

Step-2

Once you have downloaded the applicable form and filled in relevant details, an XML file (a compressed format for uploading on the Income tax website) needs to be generated.

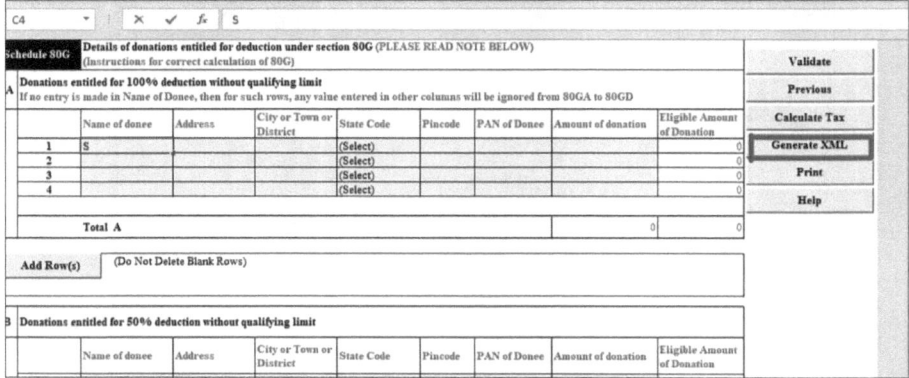

Step-3

After generating the XML file, login to the portal using your Income Tax Login ID and Password and click on **"Filing of Income tax return"** on the dashboard

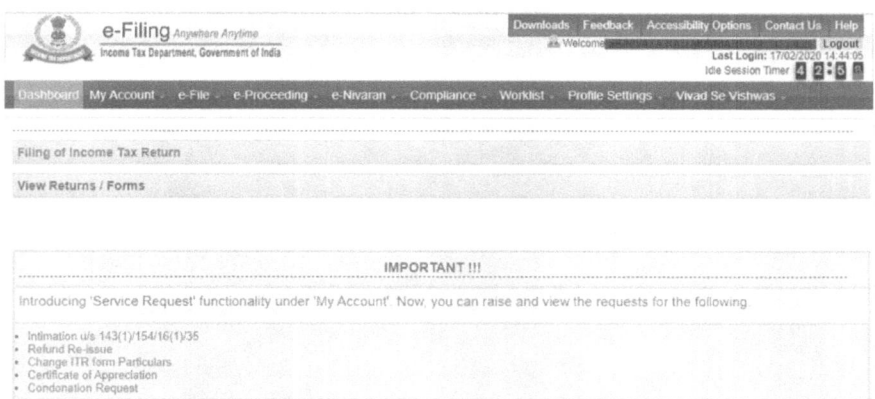

Step-4

Upload files on the Income Tax portal

Assessment Year *	2019-20
ITR Form Number *	ITR-1
Filing Type *	Original/Revised Return
Submission Mode *	Upload XML

Select one of the below option to verify your Income Tax Return

○ AADHAAR OTP (AADHAAR number XXXX XXXX 5669)-Mobile number registered with UIDAI will receive the OTP from UIDAI and it is valid for 10 minutes only. please complete the filing activity before the OTP expires. OTP will become invalid in case of logout or moving to other functionalities By selecting this option, you are agreeing to validate your Aadhaar details with UIDAI.

○ Already generated EVC through My Account -> Generate EVC option or Bank ATM. Validity of such EVC is 72 hours from the time of generation

○ I would like to e-Verify later. Please remind me

OR

○ I don't want to e-Verify this Income Tax Return and would like to send signed ITR-V through normal or speed post to "Centralized Processing Center, Income Tax Department, Bengaluru - 560 500"

[Continue] [Cancel]

6.2.2.3 Withholding taxes

We come to the opposite side of TDS – deduction of tax at source while making payments. Any person making payments exceeding certain thresholds is required to deduct tax on the same and deposit with the government as per defined rates.

TDS is deducted on the following types of payments:

- ❖ Salaries
- ❖ Interest paid by banks
- ❖ Dividend
- ❖ Commission
- ❖ Rent
- ❖ Consultation charges
- ❖ Professional charges

Once the deductor has deposited TDS with the government, details of the same also must be 'returned' quarterly using different forms.

6.2.2.4 Payment of advance taxes

We've established the core reason for taxation by a government – money needed to run the country. If all taxpayers paid taxes only at the year-end, don't you think the government would have serious cash flow problems?

This is where advance tax helps them smooth out tax collections over the year. Advance tax can be thought of as a 'pay as you earn' tax; payment of tax in installments specified by the government.

Liability to pay advance tax depends on the taxpayer:

1. **Individuals earning salary, business or profession income (under the normal scheme):** If total tax liability (after reducing TDS) is Rs. 10,000 or more in a financial year, advance tax needs to be paid. However, if you're 60 years of age or more, and do not run a business, take it easy and don't pay taxes in advance

Due Date	Advance Tax Payable
On or before 15th June	15% of advance tax
On or before 15th September	45% of advance tax less advance tax already paid
On or before 15th December	75% of advance tax less advance tax already paid
On or before 15th March	100% of advance tax less advance tax already paid

2. **Businesses and professionals who have opted for Presumptive taxation:** They must pay the whole advance tax amount in one instalment on or before 15 March

Due Date	Advance Tax Payable
On or before 15th March	100% of advance tax

If you miss the 15 March deadline, don't worry! You can still go ahead and pay advance tax on or before 31 March. Any payment of advance tax after 15 March but before 30 March is also considered as advance tax. However, interest under multiple sections starts becoming due if you don't pay advance taxes as per the above timelines. The income tax officer may also levy a penalty, not exceeding taxes due, when an assessee is in default unless they are convinced that the default was due to a reasonable cause.

6.2.2.5 Payment of self-assessment tax

Self-assessment tax, as the name suggests, is any balance tax paid after considering TDS and Advance Tax paid, before you file an ITR of income. The steps for paying the same are given below.

Step-1

Go to https://www.tin-nsdl.com/ and select **e-payment: Pay Taxes Online** under the 'Services' tab

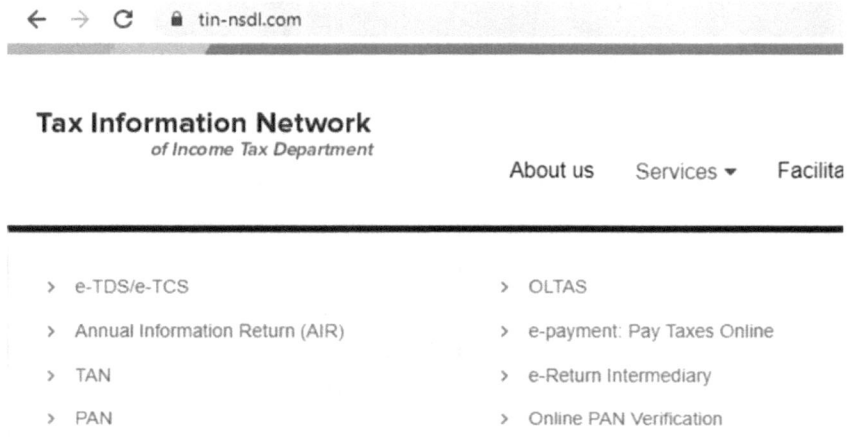

Step-2

There are various types of challans - **ITNS 280** is used for payment of self-assessment tax

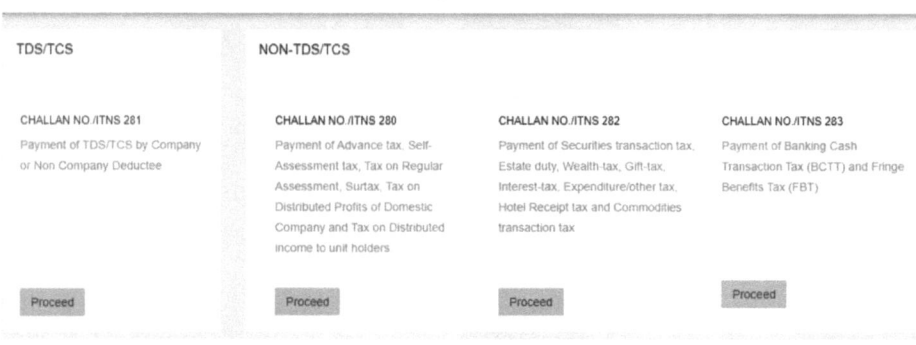

Step-3

Fill the requisite details & make payment. The payment acknowledgement should get generated.

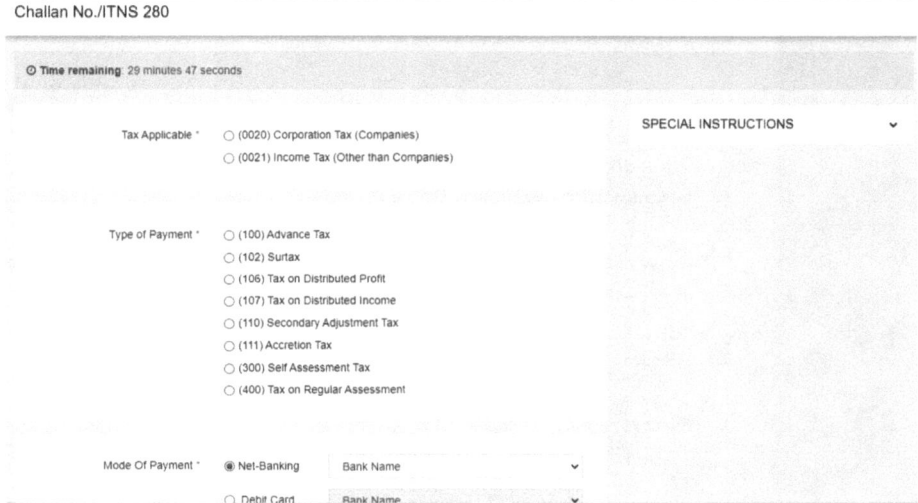

6.2.3 Receiving a notice

Receiving a notice from the Income Tax department can mean many things – so don't freak out when you get this via courier or email! Not every notice is bad for you, and it is important to understand the contents of each notice before you jump to conclusions (Exhibit 45).

EXHIBIT 45 | MAJOR TYPES OF NOTICES THAT CAN ARRIVE IN YOUR REGISTERED EMAIL INBOX

	Section	What does it mean?	What shall I do?
1	143(1)	**Intimation:** system-generated notice on your ITR tax amount vs the IT dept.'s	Verify personal details, tax amounts and correct discrepancies, if any
2	139(9)	**Defective return:** due to some mistakes at time of filing	Correct your return within 15 days from notice
3	142(1)	**Inquiry before assessment:** to understand non-filing or furnish more details	Respond within time in the notice to avoid penalties, prosecution or best judgement assessment
4	143(2)	**Selection for assessment:** detailed scrutiny to be conducted	Appear before the officer to place your arguments and evidences or submit an online response
5	156	**Pay up:** asking to make payment to the department for tax, interest or penalty liability	Respond with either of: • Correct demand • Partially correct demand • Disagree with demand • Demand is not correct but agree for adjustment.
6	131(1A)	**Summons:** Issued summons to assesses even if nothing is pending	Keep documents ready, be present physically if asked, seek extension in case of valid reason
7	148	**Income escaping assessment:** where it is suspected that income is not disclosed	File a fresh return of income as the case is reopened

Worried about the notice being valid? You also have the facility to verify its validity using the Documentation Identification Number (DIN). Any notice without a DIN is treated as invalid by the CBDT.

Step 1:

Visit www.incometaxindiaefiling.gov.in

Step 2:

Under the 'Authenticate' tab which is below the 'Quick links' tab, you will find click on 'Notice/order issued by ITD'

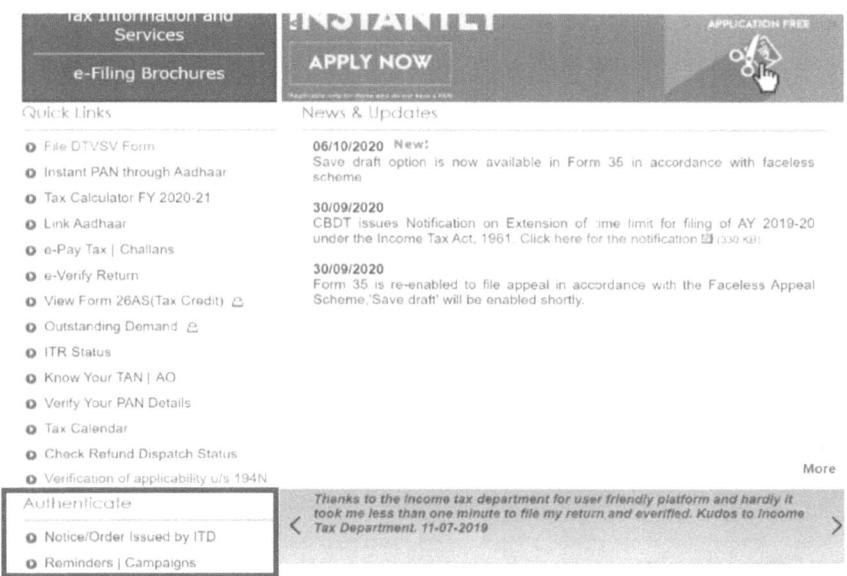

Step 3:

You can authenticate the document either by the document number or via PAN, assessment year, Notice Section, Month and Year of issue.

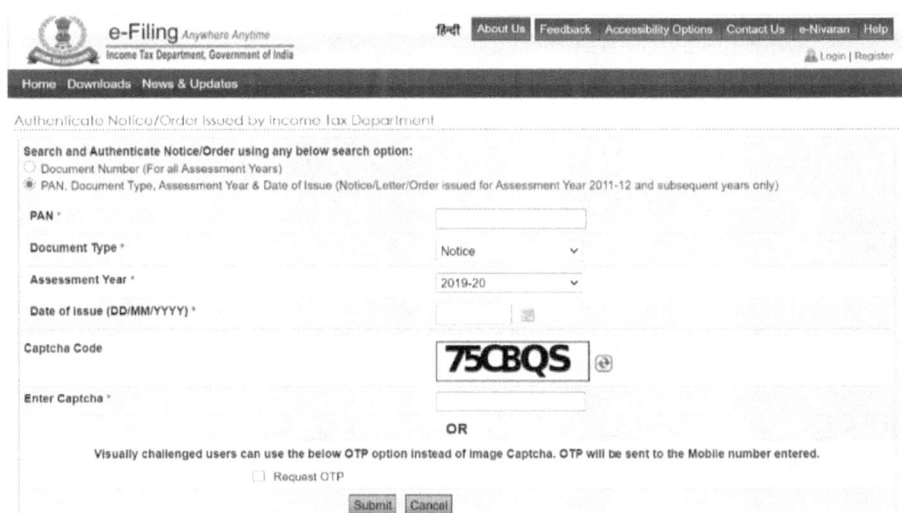

If the notice or order issued to you is genuine, then the same will be reflected on the website. The website will show you the message: "Yes, Notice is valid and issued by Income Tax Authority".

6.2.4 Replying to a notice

No need to write and post a letter to your AO. Replying to an Income Tax notice is also made taxpayer-friendly by taking it online.

Step 1:

Login to your account on the e-filing website

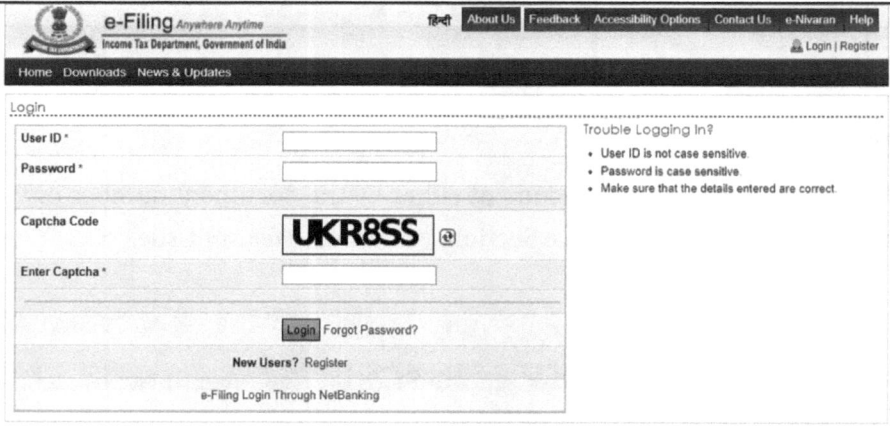

Step 2:

Click on the 'e-file' tab and select 'Response to outstanding Tax Demand' option

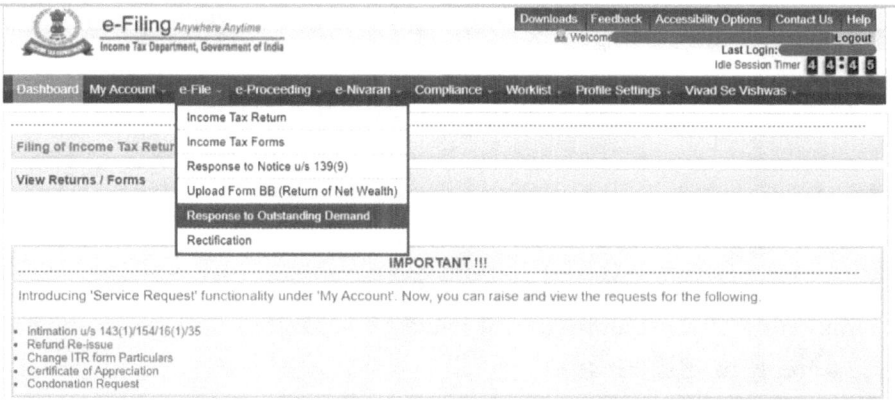

Step 3:

An outstanding tax demand notice will appear on your screen – click on 'Submit' for the appropriate year and select either of the following options:

- ❖ Demand is correct
- ❖ Demand is partially correct
- ❖ Disagree with demand
- ❖ Demand is not correct but agree for adjustment

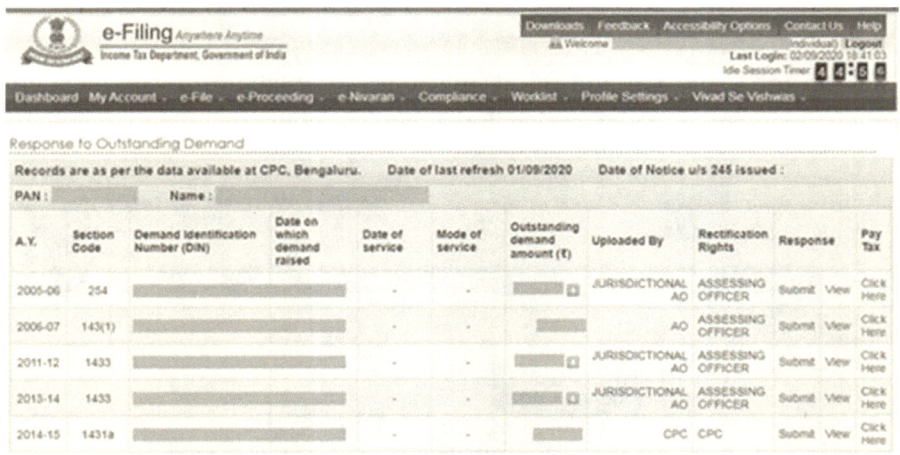

Each one of these options will trigger a separate set of questions you need to reply to (Exhibit 46).

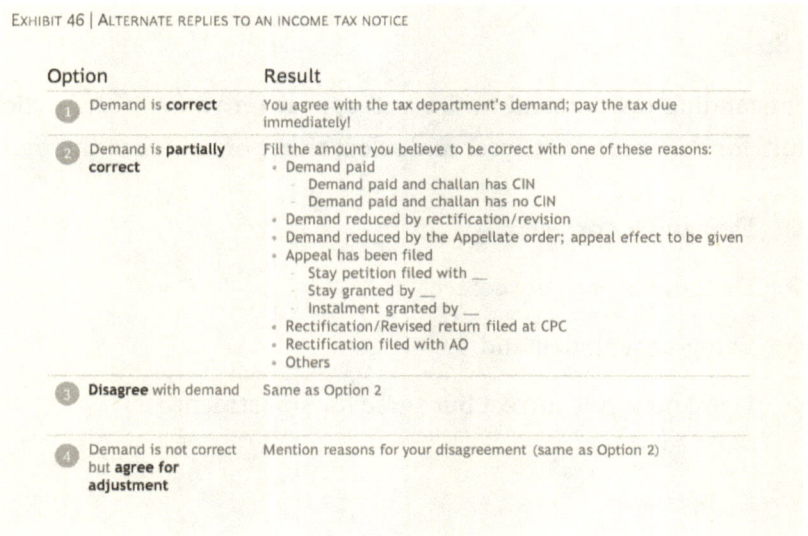

EXHIBIT 46 | ALTERNATE REPLIES TO AN INCOME TAX NOTICE

Once you submit your reply, a transaction ID is generated – check your account every 10 days and click on this ID to know the department's response!

(It is advised to perform this act with professional expertise)

6.2.5 Resolving differences

In the event the assessing officer is not satisfied with your arguments or evidences, and passes the notice demanding income tax to be paid – it becomes important to escalate things.

The Income Tax Act has provisions to appeal to higher authorities with greater power than the officers on payment of prescribed fees.

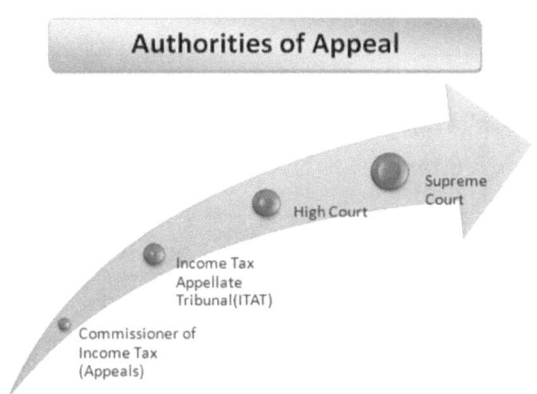

1. The first level appeal can be filed at Commissioner of Income Tax level within 30 days from receipt of income tax demand notice along with the following documents:

    a. Statement of facts
    b. Grounds of appeal
    c. Order copy

   Similarly, every appeal will have to be at an even higher level of authority, not an equal or lower level authority:

2. ITAT
3. High Court
4. Supreme Court

Vivad Se Vishwas Scheme 2020

The Budget 2020 proposed a new scheme for dispute resolution related to taxes called 'Vivad se Vishwas' and introduced the Bill in the Parliament on 5th Feb 2020. This Bill has been passed as the Direct Tax Vivad Se Vishwas Act, 2020 on 17th March 2020.

Over the years, number of appeals filed has been higher than the number of appeals disposed. This has led to pendency of appeals, and along with them, a substantial amount of tax due locked-up in those appeals (a whopping 9.32 lakh crores as on November 2019, close to one year's tax collections!). This scheme is proposed to reduce litigation and clear deadlocks in tax arrears.

Under the scheme, eligible cases under income tax pending with tax authorities can be settled at lower payment terms namely –

Payment made on or before	Appeal, writ, SLP, arbitration related to disputed tax	Appeal, writ, SLP, arbitration related only to disputed penalty or interest or fee
Original: 31 March 2020 **Current: 31 December 2020**	**100%** of disputed tax (125% in search cases) *[waiver of interest and penalty]*	**25%** of disputed interest or penalty or fee
End date (Original expectation: 30 June 2020)	**110%** of disputed tax (135% in search cases) *[waiver of interest and penalty]*	**30%** of disputed interest or penalty or fee

To make this more attractive, this was amended such that if the tax department has filed an appeal or where the issue has been decided in favor of the taxpayer (and has not been reversed by a higher forum), the amount payable shall be 50% of the above-mentioned amounts.

Originally, the scheme offered complete waiver on interest and penalty to taxpayers who settled the full dispute by 31 March 2020. Anybody who paid after 31 March up to 30 June 2020 had to pay additional 10% penalty on the disputed tax amount. However, owing to the COVID-19 crisis, the scheme was extended twice, finally till **31 December 2020** without paying any additional penalty.

6.3 Indirect tax compliances

6.3.1 Steps on GST registration

Step-1: Go to https://www.gst.gov.in/ and select 'registration' under Services tab.

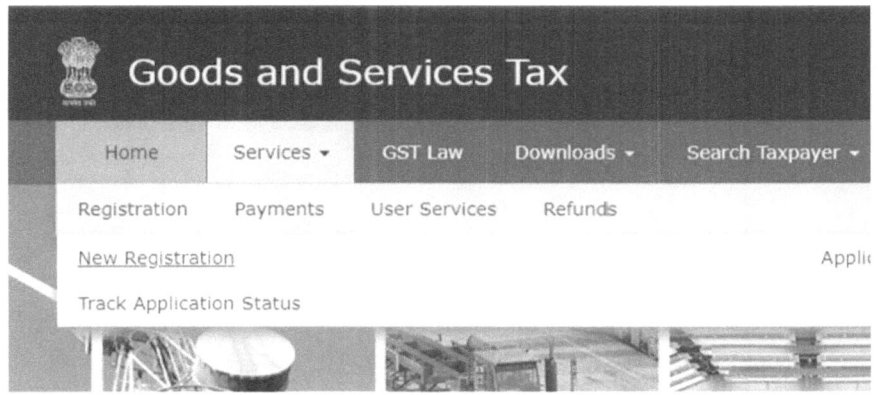

Step-2: Fill in the relevant details required below:

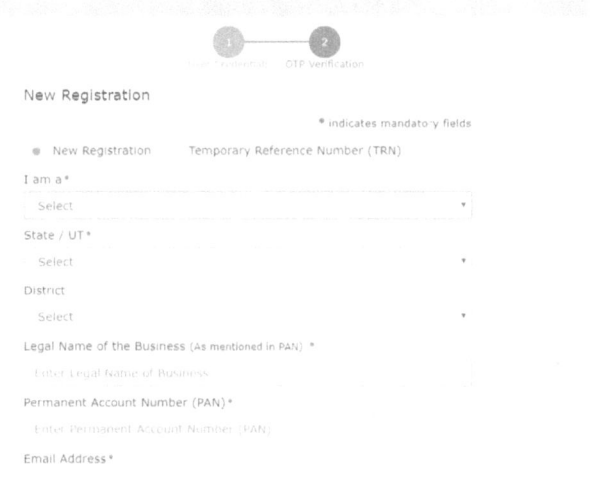

Step-3: After filling all the details, a TRN (Temporary Reference Number) is generated. Use the same to fill Part-B of the application and upload required documents.

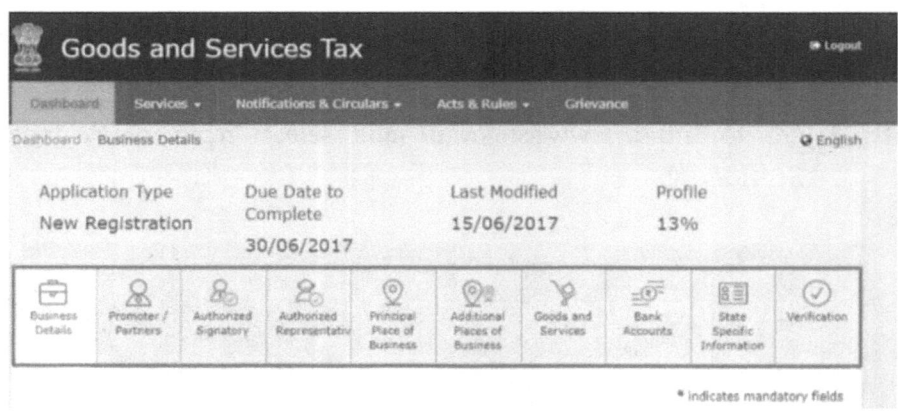

Step-4: After successfully uploading all documents and validating with an OTP in case of sole proprietary concern and digital signature in case of Company or LLP, an acknowledgement with ARN (Application Reference Number) will be generated.

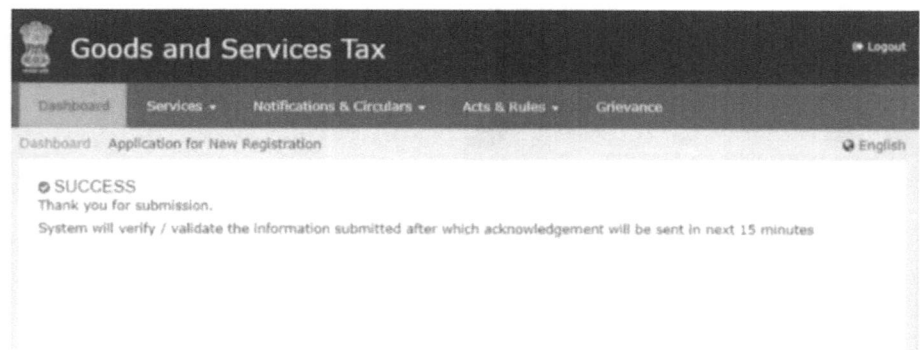

Step-5: Typically, the intimation on User ID and Password is received within 3 days from date of submission of application.

6.3.2 Steps on GST return filing and payment

GST return is a form for registered taxpayers based on their type (e.g. regular taxpayer, composition dealer, e-commerce operator, TDS deductor, non-resident, etc.). Usually, a regular taxpayer will have to file two returns per month (GSTR-1, GSTR-3B) and an annual return (GSTR-9/9C) for each GST registration separately. We have listed down the major types of GST returns and their due dates (Exhibit 47).

EXHIBIT 47 | MAJOR GST RETURNS REQUIRED TO BE FILED BY TAXPAYERS REGISTERED UNDER GST

Return Form	Particulars	Frequency	Due Date
GSTR-1	• Goods or services supplied	Monthly	11th of the next month
GSTR-1 (small taxpayers - revenue up to Rs.1.5 crore in PY)	• Goods or services supplied	Quarterly	31st/30th of the month after quarter ending
GSTR-3B	• Outward supplies, input tax credit along with payment of tax	Monthly	20th of the next month
CMP-08[1]	• For taxpayers under composition scheme	Quarterly	18th of the month after quarter ending
GSTR-8	• For e-commerce operators (that deduct tax at source under GST)	Monthly	10th of the next month
GSTR-9	• For normal taxpayers[2]	Annually	31st December of next financial year
GSTR-9A	• For taxpayers under composition scheme	Annually	31st December of next financial year
GSTR-10	• Final Return	Once When registration is cancelled/ surrendered	Within 3 months of cancellation or order, whichever is later

Note: Due dates and returns are subject to changes by Notifications/ Orders
1. Same as the erstwhile form GSTR-4, which is made an annual return with effect from FY 2019-2020 onwards
2. Not required for taxpayers under composition scheme, casual taxable person, Input service distributors, Non-residents, Persons paying TDS under section 51 of CGST Act

Demystifying Tax for the Common Man

Steps to file a typical GST returns are given below:

Step-1: After logging in to the GST website, the below screen appears.

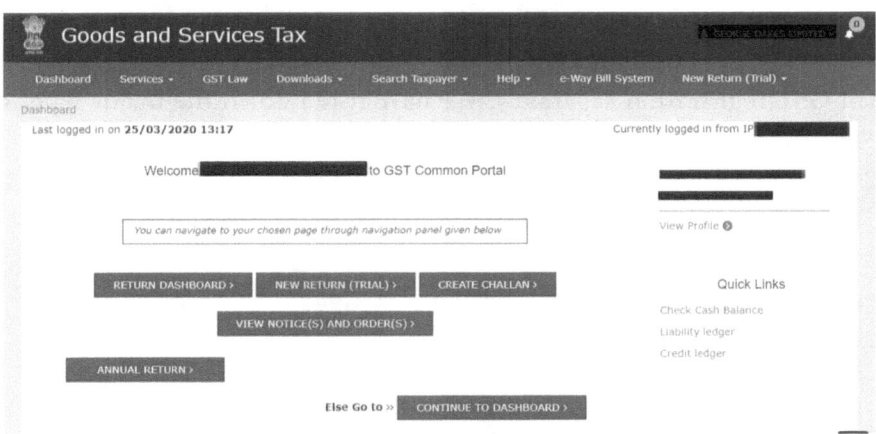

Step-2: Once you click on 'Return Dashboard' and select the return filing month, the following screen will appear:

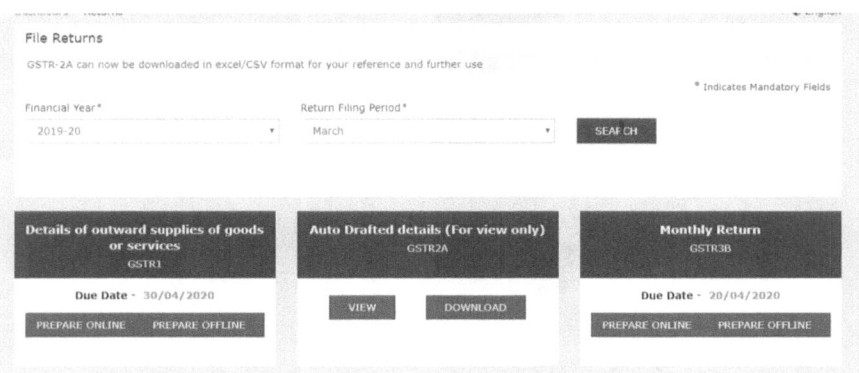

Step-3: Click on 'Prepare online / Prepare offline' and select the type of GST return to be filed. After filling the details, preview the PDF and proceed to payment.

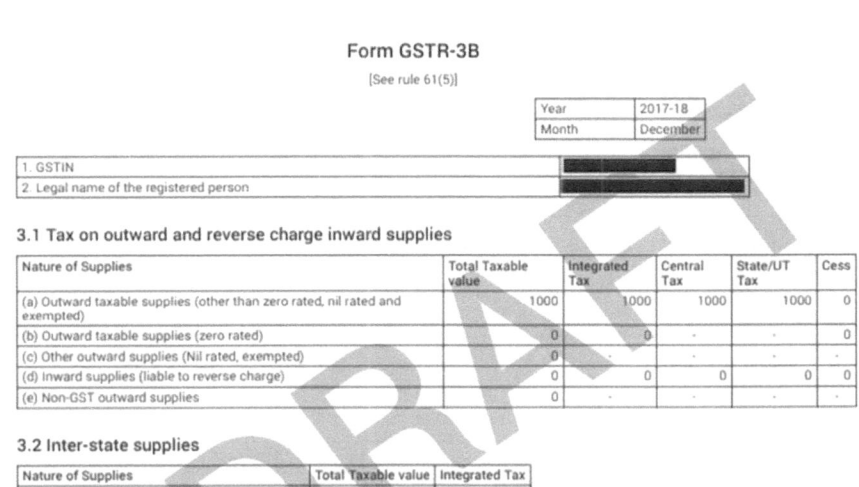

Demystifying Tax for the Common Man

Step-4: Payment receipt will be as follows:

GOODS AND SERVICES TAX PAYMENT RECEIPT							
CPIN:	Deposit Date : 19/06/2018		Deposit Time : 15:51:07			e-Scroll :	
Payment Particulars							
CIN:		Name of Bank:				BRN:	
Details of Taxpayer							
GSTIN:		E-mail Id:				Mobile No.:	
Name:		Address : XXXXXXXXX Delhi,110005					
Details of Deposit (All Amount in Rs.)							
Government	Major Head	Minor Head					
		Tax	Interest	Penalty	Fee	Others	Total
Government of India	CGST(0005)	22995	0	0	0	0	22995
	IGST(0008)	0	0	0	0	0	0
	CESS(0009)	0	0	0	0	0	0
	Sub-Total	22995	0	0	0	0	22995
Delhi	SGST(0006)	22995	0	0	0	0	22995
Total Amount							45990
Total Amount (in words)		Rupees Forty-Five Thousand Nine hundred Ninety Only					
Mode of Payment: Internet Banking -							
Notes:							

6.4 Key takeaways

EXHIBIT 48 | KEY TAKEAWAYS FROM CHAPTER 6

- Tax obligations don't just include paying tax, **multiple compliances** come with it under both direct and indirect tax

- Direct tax: To begin with, you'll need to **apply for a PAN card if you don't have one** to quote on mandatory transactions, disclose any income and pay taxes

- To run a responsible business, you'll have to **maintain proper records**, **file your ITRs** on time, **withhold taxes** wherever needed and **pay advance/self-assessment taxes** whenever due

- Receiving a notice from the Income Tax Department is normal! Don't jump to conclusions till you **understand why you have received the notice** - it could mean many things.

- Even if you are at crossroads with the Department, there are **multiple avenues to resolve differences** (appeal at CIT(A), ITAT, HC, SC, Vivad se Vishwas scheme 2020, etc.)

- Indirect tax: In order to be compliant with GST regulations, **get registered and understand which returns need to be filed and at what frequency** (make sure there's no delay!)

ABOUT THE AUTHOR

CA Viren Rajani

Viren is a buy-side investment professional at the Mumbai office of Kedaara Capital Advisors LLP. Before this, he worked at Boston Consulting Group for three years in the India, US & Europe offices where he has advised several blue chip & Fortune 500 companies. He is a rank-holder Chartered Accountant, who completed three years of his articleship with DVS Advisors LLP. He has completed all levels of the Chartered Financial Analyst (CFA) program (CFA Institute, USA) and has been teaching aspiring CFA students for more than five years. He holds a Bachelor of Commerce from Madras University, where he graduated with distinction. When not at work, he loves to travel and experience various cultures & cuisines.

TEAM

Karishma Gajaria

Karishma is a Senior Associate at Boston Consulting Group and has been working there for two years. She pursued her articleship with Ernst & Young LLP in Mumbai. She joined BCG in August 2018 after passing her CA Final exam with an All India Rank. She holds a Bachelor of Commerce from Narsee Monjee College of Commerce & Economics.

CA Chandra Sai Mathi

Chandra Sai is currently working with RGN Price & Co in Chennai. He completed his articleship with DVS Advisors LLP in Chennai and qualified as a Chartered Accountant in 2018.

www.ingramcontent.com/pod-product-compliance
Lightning Source LLC
Chambersburg PA
CBHW030807180526
45163CB00003B/1182